HOW TO GROW YOUR BUSINESS WHILE YOUR COMPETITION STRUGGLES

84 EASY IDEAS TO RECESSION-PROOF YOUR BUSINESS

Stuart Lockley

MARKLAND BUSINESS SOLUTIONS LIMITED

HOW TO GROW YOUR BUSINESS WHILE YOUR
COMPETITION STRUGGLES
Copyright © Stuart Lockley 2008

All Rights Reserved

No part of this book may be reproduced in any form,
by photocopying or by any electronic or mechanical means,
Including information storage or retrieval systems,
without permission in writing from both the copyright
owner and the publisher of this book.

ISBN : 978-095587-720-9

First Published 2008 by
Markland Business Solutions Limited

Printed in the UK by Printondemand-Worldwide Ltd

This book is dedicated to all the people I have known over the years who have, knowingly or otherwise, provided the lessons I needed to learn in order to reach the point I am at today.

PREFACE

Approximately 80% of all new businesses fail within five years of being started. Of those who survive five years 80% will fail within the next five years of life. As a result only 4% of new businesses will survive to celebrate their 10th anniversary.

So what catastrophe leads to all those shattered dreams? Perhaps the business is under financed, costs are not controlled, the product is not good enough, marketing systems do not bring in enough business. There are many possible explanations but I suspect they all come back to one problem.

What makes the difference for the business that survives?

If a company is going to survive, grow and prosper well into the future then it is essential that the owner and manager is constantly looking for, and applying new idea to his business. The world keeps changing. Every year things seem to change faster than the year before. For a business to prosper the managers must be on a constant quest for ways to improve.

There is no way you can know everything you need to know and most of the knowledge you have today will be outdated in a few years time.

Does this book contain all the answers? Of course not, but it does contain a number of very good ideas. If you only take one of these ideas and apply it to your business, the time and effort will be well rewarded.

Your business can be one of the 4% if you take action today.

Wishing you every success.

Stuart Lockley

Contents

Where Do You Start?   1

1 Know What You Want And Be Grateful For What You Have   1
2 Have A Grand Vision.   3
3 What Are You Going To Do Next?   5
4 Step Your Way To Your Goals   7
5 Is It Really Your Job?   9
6 If It Isn't Broke, Don't Fix It   11
7 Do The Best You Can At Whatever You Are Doing.   13
8 Try Something New.   15
9 Learn To Speak To An Audience.   17

Plan For Where You Are Going   19

10 Three Plans May Seem Too Much.   19
11 Conduct Regular Planning Sessions with Staff and Management.   22
12 What Is Your Contingency Staffing Plan?   24
13 What Is Happening Tomorrow?   26
14 Measure Everything.   28
15 Keep The Best, Scrap The Rest.   29
16 Learn, Learn, Learn.   31
17 Analyse Mistakes In Order To Learn From Them.   33

What Makes A Successful Entrepreneur?   37

18 Successful Entrepreneurs Never Stop Learning And Growing.   37
19 Successful Entrepreneurs Are Willing To Seek Advice.   38
20 Successful Entrepreneurs Never Give Up.   39
21 Successful Entrepreneurs Focus On Marketing.   41
22 Successful Entrepreneurs Are Willing To Test And Measure.   42
23 Successful Entrepreneurs Are Systems Orientated.   43

Ideas To Grow Your Business   44

24 Provide A First Class Service.   44
25 Survey Clients To Determine How To Better Serve Them.   45
26 Offer Clients A Bonus Not Available To Others.   47
27 Do Not Be Afraid To Sack A Customer.   49
28 Choose Clients To Fit In With Our Way Of Doing Business.   51

29 Show Your Customers You Care.	53
30 Ask Your Staff.	54
31 Ask Your Customers.	55
32 Create And Use A Marketing Plan.	56
33 Differentiating Your Business.	57
34 Don't Spray And Pray.	58
35 Market To Your Current Customers.	59
36 Following Up With Your Prospects.	60
37 Test And Track Your Marketing Efforts.	61
38 What Is Your Biggest Asset?	62
39 Keep In Touch With Your Clients.	63
40 Provide Post-Purchase Reassurance.	64
41 Give Your Clients The Best Deals You Can.	65
42 Review Your Client Base And Rank Your Customers.	66
43 Listen To Your Customers And Provide What They Want.	67
44 Put Yourself In Your Customer's Shoes.	68
45 Offer Tiered Services.	69
46 Own Your Problems; Own Your Customers.	70
47 Treat Them Right And They Keep Coming Back.	71
48 Lesson Learnt From A Shopkeeper.	73
49 Increase Your Market Reach.	76
50 Contact Your Customers.	78
51 Improve Your Lead Conversion.	80
52 Increase Average Order Value.	83
53 Increase Prices.	84
54 Tell Them What You Sell.	86
55 Create Packages.	87
56 Add Value.	88
57 Increase Your Products Perceived Value.	90
58 What You Do Shouts So Loudly I Cannot Hear What You Say	91
59 Back-End Products.	93
60 Joint Ventures.	95
61 Clients Are Easy To Lose.	96
62 Quality Of Service.	98
63 What Are You Promoting?	100
64 Marketing Never Works.	102
65 A Lesson In Perfume	104
66 Prepare To Sell.	107
67 Double In Value.	109
68 Contact Your Clients Today.	111
69 Price Is Not Value.	113

70 Know Your Customer.	115
71 Make Life A Little Easier.	117

Make Yourself Redundant 119

72 Free Yourself With Delegation.	119
73 Why Are You In Business?	122
74 What's Your Business?	124
75 Free Up Your Time.	126
76 Put Systems In Place.	129
77 Create A Plan.	132
78 Decisions Are Pushed Down The Hierarchy As Far As Possible.	134
79 Ask Your Staff	136
80 The Daffodil Principle	137
81 The World Rewards Action Not Thought.	139
82 How Much Do You Do Each Day?	140
83 Create A Real Business.	142
84 What Is Your Limiting Factor?	144

WHERE DO I START?

IDEA 1
KNOW WHAT YOU WANT AND BE GRATEFUL FOR WHAT YOU HAVE

Take a few moments and remember back to when you were a child. A favourite question adults like to ask children is, 'What do you want to be when you grow up?' The question is always meant to mean what job do you want, not what type of person do you wish to be.

When you were asked this question some of your answers may have been outrageous in their ambition such as being an astronaut, while others may have been driving a train or being a life-guard.

Often the response of whichever adult had asked the question was negative, "You will never be able to do that, be more realistic," or, "You can't do that, there is no money in it". I sometimes feel that this whole process is just designed to get children thinking in the same way as adults. Are you guilty of the same behaviour with your own children?

This whole process may be why people end up not knowing what they wish to do with their lives. Perhaps that is why so many people have a mid-life crisis. People suddenly realise they have spent the last twenty years doing something they did not really want to do but cannot remember what they wanted to do, and are now too afraid to break away and do it even if they could remember.

It may seem strange but if you wish to grow your business you must start by deciding what you want from your life and your business. Begin by deciding upon the life you wish to lead, the person you wish to become and begin building. Your business should be there to enhance your life not detract from it and your business cannot enhance your life until you know what you want from life.

While you are building the life you want, learn to be grateful and appreciative of everything that you have today, regardless of how much or how little that may be. You may be unhappy with certain aspects of your life, you may be driving a clapped-out old car and saying to yourself, "This man is mad, how can I be expected to be grateful and appreciative of that old rust bucket?" You may be correct; however I nevertheless suggest that you begin to be grateful and appreciative of everything in your life at the present time, the good, the not so good and the apparently bad. Even the apparent disasters are there for our education.

I make this suggestion for a simple reason. If you cannot appreciate and be grateful for your old rust bucket car you will not appreciate and be grateful for the shiny new Ferrari when you have it. If you are ungrateful and unappreciative of the Ferrari it will not bring you any more pleasure than the old car did. If the Ferrari does not bring you any more pleasure than the old car did, then what is the point in having it?

If you wish to appreciate the things you are going to have, you must begin by learning to appreciate the things you have, no matter how humble they may be. Begin today, begin now.

IDEA 2
HAVE A GRAND VISION.

When was the last time you allowed yourself to sit down quietly, on your own and dream a little? If you are like most people you have stopped dreaming unless you are asleep and then you are unable to remember the dream when you wake up. You have become so engrossed in the minutiae of day-to-day living that you have forgotten there might be more to life.

Once upon a time you dreamt of doing something. Try and remember what it was. Many people I speak to have a dream of retiring. If that is you, if you look forward to the day when you will be able to give up work, then I suggest that you ask yourself why.

Whatever you are doing today is your life. Why do you wish to retire from your life? Rather than looking forward to retirement as many people do, start and create the life that you want today. I am still far too young to retire but I suspect that if you are unable to enjoy your life today you will be unable to enjoy retirement.

Imagine you have a certain amount of money and can either spend it on doing something you enjoy each week or save it and go on a two-week holiday in twelve months time. What would you do? When our children were young we were short of money so gave them a similar choice. They chose the weekly activity because that would bring them pleasure all year.

It seems to me that waiting for retirement is a similar situation. You give up pleasure each week in the hope that

3

you will be happy when you retire. Unfortunately you will probably have forgotten how to be happy.

What has this got to do with growing a business? Simple really, if you are not happy and excited to be running and growing your business you will probably not grow as much as you might wish.

IDEA 3
WHAT ARE YOU GOING TO DO NEXT?

Do you have a list of things that you wish to achieve before you shuffle off this mortal coil? If not, why not? The only way to achieve anything is first to decide what it is going to be.

I know there are things you would like to do with your life. Places you wish to visit, people you wish to meet, skills you wish to acquire or things you wish to build. I am equally certain you cannot remember what they all are.

I am certain you cannot remember all the things you once wanted to do because when I first sat down to carry out the exercise below, I could not remember the things I wanted to do. At first I struggled to come up with a dozen items for my list.

We all become so used to "not being able" to do the things we wish to do that we forget what they are as a means of self preservation. Unfortunately the effect can often be to leave us with a nagging feeling of unease, a midlife crisis when the things we are doing do not feel right but we have no idea what we want to do. How many times have you had or heard a conversation similar to this snippet:

A: "I am fed up with work."

B: "What do you want to do?"

A: "That is part of the problem, I have no idea what I want to do."

The truth is, of course, that you do know what you want to do but you have denied it for so long that your conscious mind has parked the idea where it cannot cause any harm.

In truth you may find that you are perfectly happy with most of your life if you just start working towards a few of the things that you have always wanted to do.

So try this exercise now before you go any further:

Pick up three sheets of paper and put one of these headings on each:

- Things to do
- Things to be
- Things to have

Start adding items to each list and do not stop until you have at least 100. The problem most people have is they have forgotten how to dream. Do not limit yourself while making the list; just go with the flow and put down whatever you think of, regardless of how ridiculous it seems. No one other than yourself ever needs to see this list. Start now and come back when you have finished.

Returned so soon? I hope that you have three long lists. Now pick two or three items from each list. One item from each list should be something that will take a reasonable length of time to achieve while the others can be achieved fairly quickly.

Now start figuring out how you are going to do each of the items on the list.

IDEA 4
STEP YOUR WAY TO YOUR GOALS

Once you have your list of goals, write them down and begin to plan the steps you have to take in order to achieve each one. Written goals have a magic to them.

In order to establish the steps to achieve your goals start by taking one of them. Imagine you have just achieved that goal. What was the last step you took before your goal was achieved? Keep working your way backwards until you know the first step to take.

Once you have the steps written down you can begin to work on each goal, one step at a time. Each time you have taken a step you know you are a little closer to achieving your goal. That is how goals are achieved, one step at a time. While you are working on each individual step do not concern yourself with the other steps, they will arrive soon enough.

People often give up on their goals because the task seems too big or too difficult to achieve. The truth is different. The truth is that if you break your goal down into simple steps and take one step at a time then one day you will wake up to find that your task has been completed.

If you feel your goal is so big that you are unable to list all of the steps you must take in order to achieve it, please do not lose heart. Regardless of how large the goal is or how difficult it appears you will be able to identify the first few steps that you need to take. If you take those steps the next ones will become obvious and you will be able to continue upon your way. Do not be afraid to include seeking help and advice as a necessary step.

Most important of all: keep doing one step at a time.

IDEA 5
IS IT REALLY YOUR JOB?

If you are running a business or indeed part of a company it is time to look carefully at what your job is and should be. If you are like most executives and managers a large part of your time will be spent with a fire blanket over your shoulder and a bucket of sand in your hand. Large amounts of time will be spent putting out fires.

If you are spending your time fire fighting, you do not have time to think conceptually, to look at the world outside and consider the big picture. Unfortunately fire fighting just leaves you fighting another fire tomorrow and does not move the business forward. How do I know this for a fact? Because I have done what you are doing and many business owners I speak to say they do not have time to look at the big picture.

If you are fighting fires and concentrating on the day-to-day running of the business ask yourself why?

Is this really your job?

If this is your job what are your direct reports there for?

Many years ago I had the pleasure of spending a few hours talking to the finance director of a successful private company. The company had a December year-end and the time of year was mid-May. The finance director informed me that as far as the owner/manager was concerned the year had ended. He was concentrating on what the business would be doing next year and the year after that. His direct reports were taking care of this year.

The owner of this business did not start out wealthy but you may not be surprised to learn that he had created a very successful business and had become very rich.

Try this exercise:

For the next two weeks record everything that you do in six-minute units. A solicitor would do this as a matter of routine so I feel sure that you can manage. At the end of two weeks analyse how you spend your time. How much is spent on day-to-day routines, how much is spent on fire fighting and how much is spent on the *big picture* and moving the business forward?

Remember that you are giving up other things in your life, perhaps time with your family, in order to fight fires and deal with routine. Now comes the interesting part.

Analyse your routine work and establish how much can be delegated. You are the most highly paid person in your business, should you really spend all that time on routine?

Analyse each of the fires that you put out and ask a few questions:

• Who started the fire? The sad fact is we usually start our own fires either because of something we did or something we did not do.

• Who was the best person to put the fire out?

• What steps can be taken to ensure this particular, or a similar, fire does not start up again?

When you have finished this exercise use the time you have created to begin work on the *big picture*.

IDEA 6
IF IT ISN'T BROKE, DON'T FIX IT

We must all have been told at different time in our lives that, "if it isn't broke, don't fix it." This makes perfect sense. If something is working why go to the trouble of changing it? After all, any business owner has enough work to do just dealing with the things that are not working as they should.

Later in this book I will suggest you spend a substantial amount of your time setting up systems in your business. Once you have done so and those systems are working correctly, why would you spend time changing them?

Unfortunately the world, and especially the world of business keeps changing at an ever-increasing rate. Systems that meet your and your clients' requirements perfectly today may be failing in six months time.

If you would like your business to constantly be improving and developing it is necessary to be making constant improvements and changes.

Some people like change and are able to deal with it easily, while other people will resist change. I suspect the advice "if it isn't broke, don't fix it" came from someone who did not like a lot of change.

Unfortunately there is a problem with this advice. If you do not constantly make small changes and improvements in your business and your life, one day you will find the world has moved on and you have not. The changes you are forced to make will then be substantial and may be more than you can handle.

Begin a policy of constant change and improvement today and avoid the large, threatening changes later.

IDEA 7
DO THE BEST YOU CAN AT WHATEVER YOU ARE DOING.

Every life is made up of a series of little steps and small actions. If you carry out each little action to the best of the abilities you have today, then each day will be the best that you can make it.

Every big thing that we achieve is made up of a series of little steps. Putting a man on the moon was not one big step but millions of little steps and little actions. If we do each little step as well as we are able, then the big thing on which we are working will be as good as we are able to make it. If we carry out each little step with less than our best efforts then the big project will never be as good as it could have been.

You may be inclined to consider this to be a nice idea but you really do not have time to do your best on everything, there is just too much that needs to be done and not enough hours in the day. Of course you may be correct, but presumably you are doing the things you are doing because they have some long-term value to you and your business.

Now let me ask you a question. "If you do not have time to do the best job you can now, how will you find time to put things right later?"

You will be just as busy next week and next month. In fact you will be even busier if you are correcting things that you did two months ago because you did not have time to do your best first time round.

Try this exercise:

- Prepare a list of all the things you need to do in order to move your business forward.

- Separate out the most important from the routine

- Now identify the single most important thing that needs to be done today and then work on that one thing until it is complete.

- Move onto the most important item remaining on your list.

You may only clear one item off your list today – but at least it will be the most important thing that you need to do.

IDEA 8
TRY SOMETHING NEW.

When was the last time you tried something new? This idea can be applied both to your business and personal life. In your personal life when was the last time you tried something new just for the heck of it?

Our lives are largely run by habit and routine. We go out to the same few restaurants rather than try something new. We often eat exactly the same meal each time we go to one of our favourite restaurants. We leave home at the same time each morning and drive the same route. We eat the same things for lunch each day and if you were to list the number of different meals you eat each month you would be shocked at how few are on the list.

We do, of course, require a lot of routine in our lives. Without routine our minds would simply be overwhelmed by the number of decisions we have to make each day. Just driving to work each day would be exhausting if the process of driving had not become a routine.

We also need to try something new and bring a little adventure into our lives. If we never try anything new then our lives have stagnated, we have stopped growing and are really just waiting for time to pass.

Does it matter what new things you try? Probably not, unless it is guaranteed to cause you harm, such as taking drugs. Will you enjoy the new things you try? Maybe yes and maybe no, but if you never try anything new you will never know if you enjoy it. Try something new today, even if you just start with a different filling on your sandwich for lunch.

But what does this have to do with business? Well if you want your business to grow then you need to try something new. If your business is not growing or is not growing quickly enough then your marketing activities are not as effective as they need to be.

You find more effective marketing activities by trying some new ideas. If you use direct mail change the headline or change the call to action. If you do not use direct mail then try direct mail. Try advertising or try changing the adverts.

You cannot expect to achieve radically different results by continuing to do the things you have always done. If you wish to move your business forward to the next level it is time to begin testing new ideas and finding the ones that work for your business. Sometimes growing is just a matter of trying something new.

IDEA 9
LEARN TO SPEAK TO AN AUDIENCE.

The number one fear of most adults, both men and women, anywhere in the world, is speaking in front of an audience. Is this you? Do your knees knock and your palms sweat while your mouth goes dry just at the very idea? Do you stay awake the night before a presentation because you cannot stop thinking about what might happen?

If this describes you then it is time to take yourself in hand and overcome this fear. Learning to speak to a group will open up many doors that are normally closed to you. You will begin to feel more relaxed and confident in many areas of your life.

However old you are there are very few things that you can do that will have a more positive impact upon your life than leaning to speak to a group of people. This is a skill that will leave you feeling more confident in all aspects of your life. It is a skill of such rarity that once you have acquired it opportunities will arrive that you never dreamed possible.

Everybody (yes, even you) has the potential to stand up and speak to an audience with confidence. If you can speak on a one-on-one basis then you can speak to a group. Of course there are certain skills and techniques to learn but learn them you can, just as you learnt to drive.

You may be thinking you are comfortable speaking to a group and hence you do not need to give this topic any further consideration. But what about your staff? Have you stopped to consider how much your business is losing because staff are unwilling to speak to an audience?

How many good ideas have been lost because someone would not express their opinion before a group? How many good staff do you have who could be promoted if they had the increased confidence that comes from the willingness to speak to a group?

You owe it to yourself to ensure you and your staff are both willing and comfortable making a presentation to a group.

Plan for where you are going.

There are many old clichés about planning such as, 'If you are not planning for success you are planning for failure,' and, 'If you don't know where you are going, how will you know when you get there?'

There is only one thing wrong with these clichés about planning and that is – they are right.

Management needs to know where the business is going and the staff need to know that the management know where the business is going. A plan and objectives provide a sense of direction, something to move towards and measure progress against. Without a sense that the business is moving towards something, most staff begin to lose interest and just start to fill their time from nine to five.

Unfortunately planning is a vital activity that cannot be left to anyone but the people who hope to drive the business forward.

PLAN FOR WHERE YOU'RE GOING

IDEA 10
THREE PLANS MAY SEEM TOO MUCH.

Most businesses spend large amounts of time and money preparing a plan only to then file it in a drawer and forget about it. A budget is prepared and compared against the actual results each month. While things are going well relatively little attention is paid to the comparison between budget and actual results. As soon as things start to go wrong, management usually looks for a place to cut costs.

Although I would not suggest doing away with budgets, as they are important in running any business, I would suggest that your overall plan is broken down into three elements.

1 – Strategic plan.

It is essential to establish where is the business going and why. The management and staff need to have something to aim at and the sense that someone knows where the business is supposed to be going.

This element of the plan should never need to cover more than one page and usually much less. Consider where the company will be in five and ten years time.

- What size are you aiming at?
- What industry will you be in?
- Where will you stand in your industry?

- What will you be known for?
- What countries will you be operating in?
- Will you be producing a cheap or a quality product?

In one page or less it should be obvious where the business is heading. Of course, the world changes and the strategic plan cannot be written in stone. The plan should be reviewed at least every twelve months in order to ensure the business is still heading in the best direction.

2 – Management plan

Having decided where you are going it is time to decide how you are going to get there. Again each part of the plan does not need to be extensive but each department in the company must establish the things they need to be done in order to reach the target. This is not just a matter of considering sales and marketing but all of the following issues and more:

- Do you have enough space?
- Are the accounting systems adequate?
- Is the stock control system sufficient for future needs?
- What HR changes will be required?
- What training will various staff need?
- Is the recruitment process adequate?

Each department in the business must consider what it will look like when the objectives are reached and the way it will need to change. If the business is not going to be different in five or ten years' time then it will probably be falling backwards, not moving forwards.

3 – Change plan

In this plan each department must consider how the inevitable changes are going to be managed. As the business grows and develops, change is inevitable. The management of that change is an essential part of the process.

Trying to grow a business and make changes within the business without having a plan for how those changes will be implemented makes life very hard. It is essential to consider the changes to be made to all systems along with the levels of training and awareness of all staff.

All of these plans can be prepared on relatively few pieces of paper. They do not have to be immensely detailed but they do need to show the way forward. They should be clear enough so that someone who does not know the business could quickly gain an understanding of where the business is going and why, how you plan to get there and how you will manage the process.

IDEA 11
CONDUCT REGULAR PLANNING SESSIONS WITH STAFF AND MANAGEMENT.

It is amazing how many of us think we are able to do everything ourselves. I suspect this trend is worst among people who start and develop their own business.

Starting a business can be a very lonely affair. While building the business it is also necessary to overcome the scepticism of family and friends who continually counsel you against your business idea "for your own good".

Initially it is necessary to do everything yourself. A business is built from the ground up. The entrepreneur designs everything, makes everything, sells everything and designs all the systems.

As your business grows it is obvious that no one can know your business as well as you do because no one else was there at the start. Because of these influences it is difficult to let go.

I have news for you. You can only grow and create an effective and vibrant business if you:

- Learn to let go and allow your staff greater responsibility.
- Accept that your way is not the only way or necessarily the best way to achieve your objectives.

Start by involving your key staff in regular planning sessions. It is right that you should be setting the overall direction in which the company is going, but once you have set the direction and general tone of the business it is essential to involve your staff in identifying the best way to achieve your goals.

Organise regular planning sessions with your staff so that everyone knows where the business is going and what it stands for and can contribute ideas to achieve the company objectives. People like to feel valued, they like to contribute ideas and they like to feel part of something that is good, worthwhile and moving forwards.

If you involve your staff they will respond to that involvement and you will achieve your goals considerably faster with far less work.

IDEA 12
WHAT IS YOUR CONTINGENCY STAFFING PLAN?

Many years ago I was taught something very useful by a colleague with whom I worked in a large group. The person in question managed one of the branches of the company and he used to carry around in his briefcase what he called his "disaster plan".

In order to create his disaster plan he had asked himself a simple question, "What would I do if the ongoing turnover of my branch fell by 10%, or 20% or 30% next month?"

He would then create a plan so he would know exactly what he was going to do if disaster struck.

Of course he carried out this exercise because we worked in a large company with a number of branches. If his branch was severely affected by change then other branches might also be affected. While other branch managers were running around wondering what to do he would calmly open his briefcase, dust off the disaster plan and present it to his lords and masters. This way he had a good chance of keeping his own job a little longer.

You may be running your own company rather than working in a large group but this idea still has value. Times change and things go wrong. If you know the changes you will make in your business in the event that disaster should strike, then you have a far better chance of surviving and going on to prosper.

Make time to develop your own disaster plan while you are thinking about it.

Idea 13
What is happening tomorrow?

We all become engrossed in the day-to-day routine of a business, it is so easy to do and so difficult to avoid. The routine always feels urgent because it is happening now. Someone is standing in your office and needs to speak to you now. The phone rings and has to be answered now.

It is also true that if we have had a 'busy' day we feel as if we have achieved something. Dealing with the urgent and immediate produces a buzz and sense of excitement. We may go home at night feeling tired but at least we have 'achieved' something with the day.

Unfortunately when the day ends and you have spent it running around dealing with the urgent and routine matters that crop up in any business, have you actually made any progress towards your goals?

Doing the things that take you towards your goals does not usually result in lots of excitement because you are dealing with things for the future. In truth you could probably do these things next week or the week after, although that means you are simply postponing the time when you will reach your goals.

How would you feel if you set next Friday on one side to think about your business. Time to decide where you wish to be in five years time and how you are going to get there. Instead of remaining in the office you go out for the day without telling your staff where or why. Turn your mobile off and go for a walk in the country. Find a pleasant country pub for a leisurely lunch and then spend the afternoon sitting in the sun thinking about your business.

Does the very idea leave you feeling guilty? When you return home and your spouse asks about your day are you more likely to say, "I have had one of the most useful and productive days I have had in weeks," or, "Oh! Nothing much happened."

It is essential to make time to deal with the long term in your business not just the here and now.

IDEA 14
MEASURE EVERYTHING.

For most business owners and managers keeping good records is up there with systems on the list of things they least like to do. I understand this because keeping records can be difficult, time consuming and often just seems like more bureaucracy you can happily live without.

Of course you can get by without measuring everything but your business is not going to grow as fast as it could or be as effective and efficient as it could be. Only by measuring our activities will we know if the systems we have created are working as we expect and taking the business in the direction in which we wish to go.

When we measure the results of our activities we have control, we know if things are not working correctly and we are able to take corrective action. We become free to try new ideas and we are able to establish if any improvement takes place. Without measuring results we are constantly operating blind.

If you have a sales force and you wish to increase their effectiveness, begin by breaking the sales process down into its various parts and then measuring the activity and results at each stage. Once this process is in place you will be able to take action to improve sales at each stage in the process.

IDEA 15
KEEP THE BEST, SCRAP THE REST.

Many people do not like change or they like things to change only very slowly. There is nothing wrong with this but unfortunately the world of business is changing very quickly and the rate of change seems to be increasing. Any business wishing to survive and prosper must change in order to keep pace with competitors.

Change for a business means constantly improving the product or service, constantly improving the manner in which the product or service is delivered. You must be constantly looking to improve all aspects of the business. Improve your sales and marketing, after sales care, production, accounting systems, cash control, recruiting systems, in fact improve all systems.

Improving your business does become easier as you implement more systems and measure the results of those systems, partly because you are now better able to understand what is happening within your business and partly because you will have more time available to devote to improvements.

Once you have created and implemented some systems that is not the end of the matter. The world moves on and eventually improvements will be possible. When you wish to introduce new ideas test them first if at all possible then keep the best and drop anything else. For example, when conducting a direct mail campaign always send out two letters at the same time, measure the response from both and then keep the best letter to act as a control while trying to write another letter that will obtain a better response.

In order to improve you should be constantly testing and measuring then keep the best and scrap the rest.

IDEA 16
LEARN, LEARN, LEARN.

If you want your business to grow then something has to change. Perhaps your product or service needs to change and be improved. Your marketing may need improvement in order to increase the number of leads you are generating or perhaps the selling skills of your business need to improve so that more leads are converted to sales. You may need to improve your cash flow management in order to safely finance your growth.

If your business has been static or only growing slowly for the last few years you can feel certain that changes are required if you are not to be left behind by your competitors. If you are running a business or indeed part of a business the impetus for change is only likely to come from one place and that place is you.

The force for change in any organisation is usually the man or woman sitting in the top seat. Even if someone lower down the organisation is pushing for change they will have a difficult time if the head of the company is against change taking place.

Unfortunately you may be fresh out of ideas so what can you do? I suggest you start learning. We hear a lot these days about life long learning. This seems to be one of the latest fads to come out of government. Strangely enough they are right. Life long learning is important, especially if you wish to keep growing your business. If you wish to grow your business then you will require new ideas and you acquire those ideas by learning from other people.

Why would you wish to learn from other people? Because it is a lot quicker than reinventing the wheel yourself. You obtain new ideas by reading business books and magazines, going on courses, networking and discussing business or even hiring outside consultants. Many of the books you read may only provide you with one idea, many of the courses may not tell you anything new but that is not the point. If you read a book and obtain one idea you can apply in your business then reading the book was worthwhile. If you attend a course and learn one thing that you apply in your business then it was worthwhile, even if you obtain the idea from a fellow attendee rather than the presenter.

Only by seeking out new ideas and then applying them in your business will you start to grow or continue to grow. Begin and learn all you can and change your life.

IDEA 17
ANALYSE MISTAKES IN ORDER TO LEARN FROM THEM.

Mistakes are a wonderful thing, in fact they may be the best part of the day. Do you offer up a little prayer of thanks every time something goes wrong? I very much doubt it but perhaps you should.

Usually when things go wrong at work we have a million and one other things we need to do. We just do not have time to sort out one more problem. A problem is an annoyance that distracts us from more important things.

When things go wrong most people become upset or angry. We have been trained from an early age to believe that errors and mistakes are a bad thing. All of our schooling revolved around the need to be correct. A mark of 70% on a maths exam was always better than 60%. The pupils who got things right are praised and those who get things wrong are admonished.

As a result mistakes and errors are often ignored and as a result turn into far more serious problems than they were initially.

Try welcoming your problems with open arms. Treat them as the gift they are. You might like to do this for the following reasons:

- You will feel more relaxed and you blood pressure will be lower. Any business will have a stream of things going wrong, some small and some large. If you become upset at every one you are going to spend a lot of time agitated with no good result.

- If you accept problems calmly they will be reported earlier and as a result will be easier to deal with at lower cost.

- The errors and problems tell you where your systems are not working. They provide advanced warning of improvements you can make to your business and hence improve your competitive advantage. Each problem that arises gives you the opportunity to move ahead of your competitors by improving the service you provide.

All of your competitors will be facing problems of their own but most of will treat their problems as irritations. They will not learn from problems and use them to improve their business. Every day you are being presented with opportunities to move ahead and improve your competitive position.

We all make mistakes every day or at least we should be making mistakes if we are doing something. The only way to avoid making a mistake is by never trying something new and if we never try new things how can we grow, develop and become more than we are today?

The important thing, of course, is to learn something from your mistakes and then leave them behind and move on. Any mistake you make has happened for a reason and that reason is to give you the opportunity to learn something of value that you will need in order to move forward in your life.

Try giving thanks for your mistakes, embrace them, welcome them, learn the lesson they have to teach and then move onto the next mistake. Remember you will only grow your business by trying something new. Doing what you have always done in the way that you have always done it will not move you very far forwards. Whenever you try something new, mistakes are inevitable.

Enjoy your mistakes as being a sign that you are making progress.

WHAT MAKES A SUCCESSFUL ENTREPRENEUR?

IDEA 18
SUCCESSFUL ENTREPRENEURS NEVER STOP LEARNING AND GROWING.

No one can possibly know everything they need to know about running a business. As we all know, the world is changing at an ever-increasing pace and the only way to keep up with the changes is to keep learning and keep adapting. If you believe your business can be the same in five years time as it is today then I feel that sadly you are about to join the 96% who do not survive.

As it happens all business skills and behaviour can be learnt through study and practice.

Why is it so important that an entrepreneur concentrates upon his or her own education and growth?

If, at this moment, you own and manage a business turning over £1,000,000 and you wish to turn it into a business with a £3,000,000 turnover you must first be big enough as a business person to run a £3,000,000 business. As the owner and manager of the business you set the tone. If you wish to double the size of your business start by going to work on yourself and becoming a person who can manage a business of that size.

IDEA 19
SUCCESSFUL ENTREPRENEURS ARE WILLING TO SEEK ADVICE.

Trying to reinvent the wheel on a regular basis takes far too long. Certainly you may be able to find the answer to every problem on your own but how much more would you get done if you simply asked someone who already had the answer and then adapted it to your needs?

Thinking you have to do everything yourself is a good way to join the 96% club. No one can know everything and no one can do everything. Do the things you are good at and set up systems to ensure the rest gets done.

Idea 20
Successful entrepreneurs never give up.

We all have bad days; we all have bad weeks and at times we can have what seems like a disastrous year. If you wish to be successful you will face many challenges that will leave you feeling like giving up at times. Give up and you fail, it is as simple as that.

When I am having a hard time, as I do from time to time just like everyone else, I read the following poem. Why not frame it and put it on a wall in your office?

> Don't Quit
> When things go wrong as they sometimes will,
> When the road you're trudging seems all uphill,
> When the funds are low and the debts are high
> And you want to smile, but you have to sigh.
> When care is pressing you down a bit
> Rest, if you must, but don't quit.
> Life is queer with its twists and turns,
> As every one of us sometimes learns,
> And many a fellow turns about
> When he might have won had he stuck it out.
> Don't give up though the pace seems slow
> You may succeed with another blow.
> Often the goal is nearer than
> It seems to a faint and faltering man;
> Often the struggler has given up
> When he might have captured the victor's cup;
> And he learned too late when the night came down
> How close he was to the golden crown.

Success s failure turned inside out.
The silver tint of the clouds of doubt,
And you never can tell how close you are,
It may be near when it seems afar;
So stick to the fight when you're hardest hit
It's when things seem worst that you must not quit.

Anonymous

IDEA 21
SUCCESSFUL ENTREPRENEURS FOCUS ON MARKETING.

Most entrepreneurs are not trained in marketing. Most people start a business in a field they understand. Accountants start accountancy practices and mechanics start garages. Unfortunately repairing cars and preparing accounts will not bring in business. If you wish to be a successful entrepreneur you must take an interest in and become a student of marketing.

Marketing will drive your business forward because without it you will not have many clients. If you need help then get some help. Successful entrepreneurs are not afraid to seek help. Whatever else you do you must develop a marketing focus in order to succeed with your business.

IDEA 22
SUCCESSFUL ENTREPRENEURS ARE WILLING TO TEST AND MEASURE.

Whatever you are doing in any aspect of your business you can be sure of one thing: there is a better way of doing it, you just have not found it yet. Successful entrepreneurs are willing to test everything and measure the results in order to establish what works and what does not.

On most occasions, if you try something new you do not know if it will work. Test on a small scale and measure the results. If the test works then roll the new idea out. If the test is a failure try something new.

You should constantly be trying something new and improving both the business and yourself. Constant small improvements will soon move you well ahead of your competition because most of your competition will be doing the same things in the same way in two, three or four years time. Will you?

IDEA 23
SUCCESSFUL ENTREPRENEURS ARE SYSTEMS-ORIENTATED.

Michael Gerber – author of *The E Myth* – teaches us that all great entrepreneurs are systems thinkers. Your business should not be a group of people but a system run by people. The systems should do the work while the people run the system. Systems will set you free. With systems your business is not dependent upon a few key people – including you. If someone leaves they are easier to replace. If you wish to take a couple of months away on holiday the business will not collapse.

If the performance of your business is not as good as you would like stop blaming your staff and take a look at the systems you are using. With good systems in place you can work as much or as little in your business as you choose. As an added bonus you will find the systems substantially increase the value of your business when you come to sell.

IDEAS TO GROW YOUR BUSINESS

IDEA 24
PROVIDE A FIRST CLASS SERVICE.

Fortunately we all live in a competitive world. I say fortunately because competition leads to improvements in products and services and an increasing quality of life for everyone The amount of competition is increasing all the time and hence any business should be constantly improving the quality of its products in order to remain competitive. Stand still and you will be very quickly overtaken by a competitor.

Providing a service that is over and above that expected by customers may be the best way to ensure that you have long-term relationships upon which to build a business.

IDEA 25
SURVEY CLIENTS TO DETERMINE HOW TO BETTER SERVE THEM.

Most businessmen just assume they know what their clients want. Perhaps they have been in business for ten years or more and worked in the same industry before starting in business. It is natural they should know their customers, know the needs of their customers, provide a first-class service and care about their customers.

It is probably true that if you were to ask a number of businessmen then probably almost 100% would claim to know their market and know what their customers want.

If you were to then ask the same businessmen when they last asked their customers what they want, how the service could be improved and what other products or services they may require the answer is probably never or very seldom.

We all make assumptions everyday and most businessmen just assume they know their customer but do not speak to them to find out. The best market research in the world is to take your customers to lunch and get them to talk about their business. Talk about their problems and difficulties because you may be able to help solve those problems.

If one customer has a problem and you are able to provide a solution then it is very likely that other companies have the same problem and would welcome your solution.

Talk to staff at all levels in your customers' businesses to establish the things you do well and where you fall down.

The things you do well can be emphasised in your marketing literature and the areas where you fall down can be improved. If you are falling down in an area of your service and your competitors are not, they have an advantage over you.

If you improve your service in a particular area make a virtue out of the improvement and tell all of your customers. Just make sure you maintain the improved standards

Give up on the idea that you know your industry, know your customers and know their needs and requirements. The idea that you know what your customers want is costing you money and until you give up on this idea it will continue to cost you money. Speak to your clients, find out what they really want and sell it to them.

Idea 26
Offer Clients a Bonus Not Available to Others.

When was the last time you did something for your customers just to show them you care? Of course you care about your customers but unfortunately they are unaware of that. They think you are just interested in selling a few more items of your product or service in order to pay for another exotic holiday.

Of the customers you lose, most will go because of perceived indifference. They just do not believe that you care about them or their business. When your customers do not feel you care about them, it is a lot easier for your competitors to come along and sell to them.

There are many ways to make your customers and suppliers feel wanted, for example:

- Provide a special offer just for customers
- Spend some time talking to them about their business.
- Hold a raffle for tickets to a popular sporting event.
- Just send a free gift.

When was the last time you gave your customers and suppliers a gift? You may even be wondering why you would want to do such a thing. After all you supply your customers with a good product or service at a fair price and your suppliers should be grateful for your custom.

But is that really how the world works? You would not have a business without your customers and you would experience substantial difficulties if your key suppliers let you down.

One way to build a strong relationship with both groups is to give them an occasional gift so they know you are thinking about them and value your association. We all like to receive something unexpected and cannot help feeling favourably disposed towards the giver.

I do not mean a bottle of scotch although you can try that. Give your clients something that has very little cost to you but may have substantial value to them.

Among the benefits you will receive are:

1. It reminds your clients that you exist. We are all soon forgotten in the rush of everyday life.

2. It provides an excuse to phone or visit your customers, which may result in some further business.

3. You may well receive a better service from important suppliers.

4. You can use it to establish a relationship with key people amongst your customers and suppliers.

5. Your clients' businesses may improve, resulting in more business for you.

6. You will feel better about yourself.

Keep in contact with your customers and suppliers and show them that you care by doing something for them without necessarily expecting something in return. You may be surprised at the results.

IDEA 27
DO NOT BE AFRAID TO
SACK A CUSTOMER.

When was the last time you sacked a customer? Perhaps you consider this to be a ludicrous notion. After all, we all know how expensive it is to obtain new customers. When we have a customer we try to hang onto him but is that the right thing to do?

There are at least a couple of good reasons why you may wish to sack a customer.

Firstly some customers are just more trouble than they are worth. If you have a customer who constantly complains, makes unrealistic demands and is abusive to your staff, then something has to be done. You must either persuade the client to adjust their behaviour or you may be better off without them. Some clients just do not provide sufficient profit to compensate for all the aggravation they create.

Secondly there are times when you should consider sacking a perfectly good client. You have a client who purchases your product but you are really unable to provide a good service. After talking to the client it may be obvious their real needs just will not fit into your product offering. If this is the case then suggest to the client that they look for another supplier and explain why. You may even wish to suggest some alternatives.

Why would you do this if the customer is continuing to purchase from you? Simply because if you do so they will hold a high opinion of you and may recommend someone else to you If you simply continue to supply them then sooner or later you will lose them as a client anyway but probably under less than favourable circumstances.

When you sack them do so gently and continue to supply them until they find a new supplier. Treat them as you would like to be treated.

IDEA 28
CHOOSE CLIENTS TO FIT IN WITH YOUR WAY OF DOING BUSINESS.

Do you choose your clients or do you take all that you can get? Can you even afford to be choosy? After all, you need to replace the clients you lose and then you need further clients in order to grow. Does it even make any sense to be choosy about the clients and customers you take on? I think it does.

You have a way of doing business that suits your organisation. If you take on clients and customers who are comfortable doing business your way, you will have happier clients, happier staff, a more efficient and effective organisation and greater profits.

If you take on a client who will not fit into your way of doing business they will be unhappy with the service you provide and will inevitably leave. Unfortunately a client who leaves under unhappy circumstances does not make a good advertisement for your business.

Take on clients who fit your way of doing business and they are far more likely to be happy with your service and recommend you to other clients who will benefit from your service.

This approach will also help you to focus your marketing efforts. Begin by defining your ideal customer, the customer who will most benefit from your service and fit into your way of doing business. Then direct all of your marketing effort in their direction.

Once you know who you are targeting, all marketing will become more effective at a lower cost.

Of course there is one caveat to all this. If your way of doing business does not suit any potential clients then you need to change your way of doing business.

IDEA 29
SHOW YOUR CUSTOMERS YOU CARE.

The marketing genius Jay Abraham recently conducted a survey among successful growing businesses. What he found is really quite shocking. Less than 25% of these successful companies had in place a programme to systematically follow up with customers and extend further services to them.

No attempt was made to nurture them into loyal long-term clients. In fact very few of these successful companies **EVER** wrote to a customer after the sale. Successful businesses are just taking their customers for granted.

Why is this so staggering and why will it damage your business if you are following their example? Just consider the information below and you will realise why:

Reasons for customers leaving:

1. Move away or die   4%
2. Other company friendships 5%
3. Price competition   9%
4. Product dissatisfaction 14%
5. Perceived indifference   68%

If you ask most business owners or managers why they lose customers the answer will often be 'price'. In fact this is usually just not true. As many as 82% of the customers are lost because of reasons you can control. What are you doing to show you care about your customers?

IDEA 30
ASK YOUR STAFF.

If you want some ideas for improving your business ask your staff. I do not mean simply putting up a suggestion box and paying lip service to their ideas. Really ask them. Get together as a group one lunchtime, order some pizzas and ask their opinion. I guarantee your staff knows a number of ways to improve your business but they will only tell you when they believe you are interested and will take some action about their suggestions.

IDEA 31
ASK YOUR CUSTOMERS.

Most business owners never get around to asking their customers what they want. Your customers will tell you how to improve your products or service along with other products you can sell them. Go and speak to your best customers. Find out why they buy from you, what you can do to improve your product or service from their point of view, what value you can add without it costing you a great deal. Now find other companies similar to your best customers and target your marketing towards them.

IDEA 32
CREATE AND USE A MARKETING PLAN.

It is strange how people who should know better fail to produce a marketing plan. Often those who do produce a plan let it languish in the bottom drawer well out of sight.

Various studies have shown that small businesses that create and consistently use a marketing plan will achieve on average 30% higher sales than a competitor. Would you like an increase of 30% in sales?

Here are a few ideas to help you create a plan.

Tip 1 – start by identifying the reasons why your clients purchase from you.

Tip 2 – create a message that focuses on the answer to Tip 1.

Tip 3 – Break your plan down into mini-plans to cover your various sources of business.

Tip 4- Hold weekly meeting to review the plan.

IDEA 33
DIFFERENTIATING YOUR BUSINESS.

Everyone likes to belong to a group and finds comfort in being like other people. Unfortunately, if your business is to stand out then it is necessary to differentiate it from other businesses in your industry. Your prospects receive thousands of marketing messages every day and it is necessary to make your message stand out from all of that clutter.

Create your own unique selling proposition (USP) or extra value proposition (EVP).

To do this speak to your staff, customers and competitors to find out what sets you apart, then use that in all your marketing.

IDEA 34
DON'T SPRAY AND PRAY.

As difficult as this is to accept, not everyone is a good prospect for your product or service. If this is true why would you want to spend your marketing budget on trying to reach people who are never going to be interested?

Unfortunately many companies spend their money indiscriminately on advertising in radio, newspapers and magazines and pray that enough people will see the message and respond.

Why not try a different approach. Identify all of the industries in which your clients currently operate. Then identify companies in those industries and approach them directly. It is very likely that your response rate will increase and your cost per lead will go down.

IDEA 35
MARKET TO YOUR CURRENT CUSTOMERS.

Most business owners spend large amounts of time and money trying to attract new customers but ignore the gold that is already sitting in their business. Some very large companies, who should know better, also take this approach as you will be aware if you have had a mortgage where the fixed period came to an end recently.

There are two types of sale that you can be making to your existing customers.

Sale 1 – Sell them some different but related products. People like to buy from people they know, like and trust. Presumably your existing customers know, like and trust you because they are buying from you. They are already a warm lead so sell them something else.

Sale 2 – Sell them on the idea of giving you a steady stream of referrals. Your clients would like to give you a referral so do them a favour and ask. You might be pleasantly surprised at the result.

IDEA 36
FOLLOWING UP WITH YOUR PROSPECTS.

Various studies have been carried out to show that most sales take place on or after the sixth contact. If you do not follow up with your contacts you have wasted your time and money prospecting in the first place. You may just as well set your morning shower running but not bother to step under the water.

Develop a follow-up marketing campaign that can be automated as much as possible. Systematise the process using a contact management system and ensure that you follow up all your leads.

IDEA 37
TEST AND TRACK YOUR MARKETING EFFORTS.

I know half the money I spend on advertising is wasted. Now, if I only knew which half.

John Wanamaker.

Only by tracking, recording, measuring and testing is it possible to know which of your marketing efforts are working. Some things you try will succeed while other things are complete duds. It is painful to keep spending money on a campaign that you think is working when it is not.

Measure everything that you do, test various ideas in a small way first and then be prepared to modify them in order to improve.

IDEA 38
WHAT IS YOUR BIGGEST ASSET?

Whenever someone stops to consider what is the biggest asset in their company they may think in terms of plant and machinery, factory buildings or offices. It is fashionable to say that the company staff is the biggest asset but is this true? Try losing one or two of your largest clients and then decide what is the biggest asset of your company. Without clients there is no business.

In all businesses repeat buyers provide the best profit stream. They are easier and cheaper to sell to and will generally purchase more than a new customer. Long-standing customers know how to make hassle-free use of your services. They are familiar with your business and feel knowledgeable about the goods and services you provide. Many customers will value an established relationship, will be reluctant to go elsewhere and may even be prepared to pay a slight premium. The longer your customers remain with you the wealthier you will become.

Unfortunately most business people ignore their biggest asset. If you doubt this is true wait until the fixed period runs out on your mortgage and then see what kind of offer your lender will give you. Most lenders reserve their best offers for new customers. These are large, sophisticated businesses that spend hundreds of thousands to hire the best marketing brains and then spend millions on marketing and they still abuse their best asset. Do not fall into the same trap.

IDEA 39
KEEP IN TOUCH WITH YOUR CLIENTS.

Contact a new client within 48 hours of their first purchase to ensure that they are happy with the product. Then send a 'thank you' note to each new client for bringing you their business. Very few, if any of your competitors will carry out these simple steps.

On an ongoing basis you should keep in touch with your current and past clients on a monthly basis. If they do not hear from you they will forget all about you.

IDEA 40
PROVIDE POST-PURCHASE REASSURANCE.

Each time a client makes a purchase from you contact them to see how things are going. Do not wait for problems to come to you because not everyone will contact you; they will just go elsewhere. Show your customers you care and that you will resolve any problems quickly. Prove to your customers that you are genuinely interested in them not just yourself.

IDEA 41
GIVE YOUR CLIENTS THE BEST DEALS YOU CAN.

Many companies feel that they should give the best deals to attract new clients and then push the price up for existing and loyal clients. In fact you should let your existing clients have your best deals first and be sure they know that is what you are doing. Allow existing clients a special price from time to time in order to say 'thank you'. If you are going to hold a sale then let your existing clients have the first chance to purchase. Give your existing clients something others cannot obtain and you will improve loyalty.

IDEA 42
REVIEW YOUR CLIENT BASE AND RANK YOUR CUSTOMERS.

Group your customers as platinum, gold, silver and bronze. This grouping can be in terms of turnover or gross margin. To find your best clients, determine how long each has been with you, how much they've spent during the year, how much hand-holding they've required in staff time and money.

Do not assume that a large expenditure means a great customer. A big spender who eats up staff hours may not be worth more than a smaller fry who efficiently places orders and never demands special favours. Customers who are perpetually dissatisfied, always demanding and abusive toward your staff may not be worth keeping.

Now, what are you doing for your best clients to keep them happy and how are you going to turn your gold clients into platinum?

IDEA 43
LISTEN TO YOUR CUSTOMERS AND PROVIDE WHAT THEY WANT.

The first rule of a successful partnership may be old-hat but is nonetheless key. Regularly keep in touch and always listen carefully. Unhappy customers rarely complain, at least to the source of their troubles. They simply vote with their wallets. Talk to your customers in order to find out their needs and their complaints. When a customer makes a complaint you should thank and reward them in some way because they are doing you a great favour.

If you want to carry out a more serious customer-satisfaction survey, make sure you do it correctly. That means hiring an independent party to conduct a phone poll, using a sample that is a reliable cross section of your type of clients.

IDEA 44
PUT YOURSELF IN YOUR CUSTOMERS' SHOES.

The best way to forge connections with customers is to understand their business so well that you can offer comprehensive solutions to their problems. The aim is to show you care enough to make your client look terrific in front of his own customers. Consider spending time at a big customer's premises, meeting with the Chief Executive or whatever it takes to understand their business. This is the difference between saying, "Here's what I'm trying to sell you," and "Here's how much better your life will be when we're up and running."

IDEA 45
OFFER TIERED SERVICES.

Excellent overall service for all customers must be your mission. But you can still segment your market and charge a premium for special or more costly requests. Although tiered-level service may be new for you, other industries such as airlines have been doing it for years. Just be sure that everyone understands the different level of service and what they are getting for their money. Then ensure that each service level is very good value for money.

IDEA 46
OWN YOUR PROBLEMS,
OWN YOUR CUSTOMERS.

From a sales point of view there can be few things worse than losing your customers' confidence. Yet, as we all know, no one's perfect. So what do you do when you make a mistake? First, own up to it. Then, make up for it. Most customers accept that mistakes happen and things go wrong. The real problem comes when the issue is not addressed. If you move quickly and effectively to fix a customer's problem, you may even turn the mistake into a great opportunity to increase customer loyalty. If you solve the problem quickly your reputation and profile might actually be enhanced in the customer's eyes.

Finally, draw lessons from the experience. The most useful and instructive learning comes from the recognition and analysis of mistakes. Remember there is no such thing as failure, just an opportunity to learn. Unfortunately, many managers prefer not to look back.

Look at your business today and begin to capitalise on your biggest asset before you lose it.

IDEA 47
TREAT THEM RIGHT AND THEY KEEP COMING BACK.

It has taken me many years to learn a simple lesson. There are very few things in life that we are able to directly change. We cannot change our colleagues, the Government, the weather or our customers. We cannot change our spouses or our children. If we wish to influence any of those things we must begin by changing ourselves.

If you work in any organisation there are probably co-workers who you do not get long with as well as you might. No doubt they annoy and irritate you. But have you stopped to consider what might happen if you treated them differently? Would they react to you differently and become less annoying and nicer people? Perhaps it is worth a try, maybe they react towards you in the manner they do because of the way you behave towards them.

Often it is easy to blame someone else for a situation in which we are equally to blame ourselves. Even if a situation is not our "fault" it is still probably worth changing our own behaviour towards someone else if that will produce an effect that we want. Even if the change just leaves us feeling better within ourselves knowing that we have done whatever we were able to do to improve things.

How do you treat your customers? When was the last time that you sent them a simple note to say "Thank you for your custom and support", have you ever sent such a note? How would you feel towards a supplier who sent you such a letter?

When was the last time you asked your customers if there was anything you could do for them? I do not mean as a veiled message, which really means, "Is there anything else we can sell you?" Simply and genuinely ask if there is anything you can do for them without expecting anything in return.

Will some people take advantage? Probably but I am afraid that is just life. Those people were always going to take advantage in some way. What is important is the goodwill you generate among the majority of your customers. If your customers feel that you care about them they are far less likely to change supplier and will probably purchase more from you. It will always be cheaper to keep existing customers than to find new ones.

Why not just try the idea out with a few of your best customers and see what happens?

IDEA 48
LESSON LEARNT
FROM A SHOPKEEPER.

I recently had a very interesting experience while out shopping. My daughter had requested that I purchase three lever-arch files for her while I went about my lawful business and as a result I found myself in a small stationer's shop.

I picked up the files and stood at the counter waiting for my turn to be served. I became aware of a disembodied voice repeating, "They are two for £2.50." At first I just ignored the intrusion but eventually I looked around and realised the voice was, in fact, talking to me.

"They are two for £2.50." I am sure you are correct, I thought, but why are you telling me? I finally realised that the gentleman concerned meant that the lever-arch files were two for £2.50 and was asking whether I would like to purchase four rather than three.

You may be wondering why I bother to report this little encounter. The reason is simply that there are valuable lessons to be learnt that can be applied to your business regardless of size or the products/services that you supply. What are a few of these ideas?

1. Before you are able to deliver an effective sales message it is necessary to gain the attention of your prospect. In the example above a simple "Excuse me sir" would have sufficed. How do you attract the attention of your prospects? Until someone is listening to you, your

sales message is wasted regardless of how good it may or may not be.

2.   No one purchases at the first contact. It would be wonderful if contacting a prospect once would lead to a sale but unfortunately the world does not work that way. Most people will not purchase until the sixth, seventh or eight contact. This is why sending out one direct mailing piece is rarely as successful as multiple contacts over a period of time.

3.   One thing the shop owner was doing right was to up-sell at the point of sale. By offering two lever arch files for £2.50 he increased the chances that customers would make a larger purchase. What products or services are you able to bundle together and produce an irresistible offer for your customers?

4.   Measure, measure, and measure. The shop owner priced his offer in such a way that he could easily lose money if a reasonable number of customers would usually purchase two lever-arch files anyway. Had I thought to ask, I suspect it is unlikely he would be able to tell me how many files would generally be purchased at one time. Without this information it is impossible for him to know whether he is making or losing money on his offer.

5.   Contact your customers and let them know when you have a special offer. Create special offers just for your most valuable customers. This would be difficult for the shopkeeper in the example because he made no attempt to capture my name or contact details. If you do not keep your information in front of your customers you will be forgotten.

It is really very interesting just how much there is to be learnt from one little encounter in a shop while purchasing a few lever-arch files.

IDEA 49
INCREASE YOUR MARKET REACH.

You need more exposure among your targeted audience. Your business needs to be *in front of* as many potential customers as possible.

Out there somewhere are all the potential customers who could possibly be interested in your product or service.

There are a maximum number of people who have the potential to do business with you. It is your job to find as *many of them* as possible.

Most businesses are trapped in a prison of their own making. It is a prison that says they have to market in the same way as everyone else in their profession or industry. The big problem with this approach is that you are always playing catch up with everyone else. Your time is spent trying to do the same thing as everyone else a little better than everyone else.

When you market in the same way as everyone else the competition is stiff. Like it or not, if everyone in your industry is doing the same thing it is difficult to stand out.

Let me give you an example that has nothing to do with commerce although it is relevant to your business. When I was at school I learnt a valuable lesson that I am just beginning to relearn.

I did A-levels in history, economics and maths. Whenever I had to take an exam I would deliberately choose the hardest questions. I did not take this approach just because I am awkward, which I may be, and certainly not because I was very good at these subjects.

I realised a simple fact. If I chose the hardest questions there would be less competition. Fewer students would complete those questions, the marker would have fewer papers to compare mine against and I would find it easier to obtain a good mark.

The strategy seemed to work and will work for your business. Do something no one else in your industry is doing.

If you are like 95% of the business owners in this country you use just one or two methods of marketing your business, and those methods are the ones used by everyone else in your industry and you even use them in the same way as everyone else in your industry.

What would happen if, over the next few months, you added another one or two methods of marketing and then added another one or two methods so that eventually you were using up to 10 main methods of obtaining leads rather than just two.

I'll tell you what will happen. You will achieve what everyone will tell you is impossible. You may well increase your profits by 50% or 100% or possibly even more.

IDEA 50
CONTACT YOUR CUSTOMERS.

Let me give you a simple example. When was the last time you received an e-mail or a phone call from your dentist? The last time I received a call was the day *after* I had missed an appointment.

What if he decided to take my e-mail address and send me the occasional e-mail to let me know what is going on in the world of dentistry and then contacted me a couple of days *before* my appointment.

His profits would rise just because of fewer missed appointments and he could also seek referrals. I am sure his profits would rise just from following this simple strategy and he already has a receptionist who could do the work.

There are many ways any dentist could use to market his practice and enhance the value he is providing to his customers.

Look through the following marketing methods. If you are serious about growing your business choose one that you are not already doing or not doing well and add it to your marketing mix. Once you are achieving results add another method.

- Direct Mail
- Internet Marketing
- Advertising
- E-mail Marketing
- Networking
- Strategic Alliances

- Seminars
- Telephone Marketing
- Direct Sales
- Public Relations
- Referral Systems

Are you prepared to do something different and reap the rewards or would you prefer to continue doing what you are already doing and feel comfortable with? If you take a few of the methods above and implement them do you think you could increase your leads by 10%?

If so, you will be well on your way to increasing your profits by a significant amount.

IDEA 51
IMPROVE YOUR LEAD CONVERSION.

As you will have realised bringing in more leads is great, but not if you are failing to convert them into paying customers. Leads cost you money and the fewer you convert the more each new customer has cost you.

Simply obtaining lists of prospects is not enough. The real challenge is to manage the process of qualifying, managing and nurturing leads from initial contact to closure.

Lead management is important for any and every business. Any situation in which the company would follow up a customer enquiry can be improved. Most businesses will spend large amounts on generating leads only to waste most of that expenditure when the leads are not converted.

Simply making a 5% improvement in your conversion rate will make a substantial improvement to your business at very little cost.

But where do you start?

If you truly wish to improve your lead conversion then you have to be willing to measure what is happening. In most cases it can be many months before managers detect that a business is "off track" from where they expect it to be. This happens because managers do not measure the process.

At some time everyone has heard the phrase: 'If you do not measure it you cannot manage it'.

There is a lot of truth tied up in these few words, unfortunately most people choose not to act upon them.

Measuring a process enables you to detect problems early on and correct them before they become serious. So how are you going to improve your conversion rate?

Every lead goes through a process in order to be turned into a paying customer.

Just as we have broken the whole marketing process down into stages we can also break the conversion process down into stages. Breaking down the process into stages will enable us to create a sales map. A sales map will enable us to measure the results of our actions and hence be able to make changes to improve things.

The basic sales process for our example company will be in five stages.

- Lead Generation
- Conversation
- Appointment
- Proposal
- Sales

1. Following some kind of lead generation a conversation takes place with the new prospect.
2. An appointment is made.
3. If the appointment is successful a proposal will be submitted
4. From the proposals – sales are made.

Every time an action takes place it must be measured.

Small changes can have a huge impact upon your business.

But how do you know what works and what does not work?

This is where you try different ideas and test them. For instance, did you know that a salesman wearing a blue suit will sell more than if he were wearing a brown suit?

Did you know that a salesman with a beard will sell more if he has a shave?

Test ideas, find what works then make use of that.

Improving the training of your staff, offering a better guarantee and improving presentation skills can all improve conversion rates in your business.

Your goal is to make small improvements at every stage rather than large improvements at one stage.

IDEA 52
INCREASE AVERAGE ORDER VALUE.

Now you have started to obtain more leads and improve your conversion rates let's take a look at how much each order is worth. The average order value can easily be calculated as follows:

Average Order Value = Sum of Revenue Generated/Number of Orders Taken

Increase the average order value and you will not only increase your turnover but your profits will rise by a greater percentage. Why? Simply because you will have a more-or-less fixed cost of fulfilling an order. If the order value increases then more gross margin will be available after costs have been covered.

Do the maths for your own business. Calculate the fixed costs of fulfilling an order. Do not forget to include the costs of taking the order, sending out an invoice, credit control and banking the cash. When you have picked yourself up off the floor, consider looking for ways to reduce that figure.

Increasing the average order value is important because you are now selling to existing customers and we all know it is easier and cheaper to sell to an existing customer than to obtain a new one. Nevertheless most business owners spend most of their sales and marketing effort in attempting to acquire new customers.

IDEA 53
INCREASE PRICES.

How long is it since you last increased prices? Price always feels like a problem and most people are reluctant to increase prices. The sales force never wants a price increase because they perceive their jobs will become more difficult.

In fact you will rarely lose customers because of a modest price increase. This is of course a broad statement and there are commodity industries where price is a sensitive issue but this is not true for many businesses and industries.

A small increase can have a wonderful effect upon bottom line profits. Do you think your customers would pay a 1% increase in prices? If your net profits are currently running at 5% of turnover then a 1% increase in sales price will increase your net profits by 20%. Do you consider that to be an increase worth having?

If you can manage a 1% increase what about 2%? If you are concerned about increasing the price then look for ways to increase the value you provide to the customer at very little cost to yourself. Increase the value and you can increase the price. Start by asking your customers what they would like.

I must confess to learning this lesson by accident. A company I worked with in the past needed to raise prices by 20% in order to avoid bankruptcy. Everyone involved in the management of the business complained that clients would be unwilling to pay the increase but the choices were simple.

Prices were increased and the business moved from a loss to a profit. Not one client mentioned the increase in prices.

At the same time prices were increased I introduced some paper-and-ink information which, quite by accident, provided clients with something they had wanted for a long time. A number of clients mentioned the added value while no one mentioned the price increase.

Could you do something similar?

IDEA 54
TELL THEM WHAT YOU SELL.

Most companies never keep their customers informed about the products and services they provide. If you have more than 10 products or services there is a very good chance that no one in your company is able to sit down with a blank piece of paper and name them all.

If you do not know your product range what chance is there your customers know everything you sell. Customers will only purchase what they know you sell. Start today and begin a systematic programme to keep your customers informed about your product range.

If you do not have a range of products, now is the time to start thinking about developing one.

IDEA 55
CREATE PACKAGES.

Consider creating a package of products for customers which provides good value while increasing your average order value. Once a customer has made the decision to purchase, that is the time to offer a bundle of products or to up-sell with a special offer.

This is why supermarkets display impulse items near the checkout. Customers have already made a purchase and while they wait to pay they have the opportunity to examine items that are low cost and can be purchased on a whim.

Consider what happens in the very simple example below. A customer has just purchased product A that sells for £100 and produces a profit of £50. Now you offer a bundle of product A and product B. Product B also sells for £100 and produces a profit of £50 but you sell the two together for £180.

Turnover on this order has now increased by 80% and profits have increased by 60% while your costs of processing the order are probably unchanged.

	Product A	Products A & B
Sale Price	100	180
Cost	50	100
Profit	50	80
Increase in profit		**60%**

Could you do something similar in your business?

IDEA 56
ADD VALUE.

One of the primary tasks in your business is to add value to the customer experience. When you receive excellent service you always feel better about a company and when the service is poor you are indifferent to a company at best and may immediately begin to look for another supplier.

When you receive an outstanding service you are more likely to want to talk to and about your supplier. You are less likely to quibble about price and more likely to pass on referrals.

Start and run your business so that it treats customers in the way you would like to be treated. Constantly look for ways to improve the experience of everyone who comes in contact with your business.

When considering service levels most business owners simply consider the service provided to customers. In fact if you wish to have a first class business you must also consider your suppliers.

Many companies delay payments to suppliers and quibble about the quality of goods supplied or whether they have been supplied at all. At the same time the company will be expecting customers to pay on time and complaining when they do not.

When you delay payments to suppliers you set up the idea that payments can be delayed to you. If you do not already do so begin to pay your suppliers promptly and efficiently before they chase for payment and then insist your customers do the same for you.

Delaying payment to suppliers and insisting customers pay promptly lacks integrity and a business needs integrity to keep a good long term relationship with all its partners.

IDEA 57
INCREASE YOUR PRODUCTS PERCEIVED VALUE.

You can dramatically increase the profits of your business by increasing the perceived value of your product or service. Often this can be achieved cheaply and with relatively little effort.

You may remember the example I gave earlier about increasing prices and how I achieved a 20% increase for a company with no complaints from customers. This was achieved by increasing the perceived value of the service.

The company was in a niche industry that was not very good at explaining to customers the work they did – work that could stretch over a couple of years. Being new to the industry I wanted to understand the process and I put together some simple information to help clients budget for the costs involved.

I had to make things simple so that I could understand the process, and as a result the clients were able to understand. Many said that having read the new information they felt they understood what was happening for the first time. This is a very low cost, high value approach. How can you use it?

IDEA 58
WHAT YOU DO SHOUTS SO LOUDLY I CANNOT HEAR WHAT YOU SAY

I am assuming you have a Unique Selling Proposition (USP) for your business. If not I suggest you develop one. The problem comes when companies use the USP as a sales aid and then forget about it once they have a customer on board.

Your USP must run throughout all the activities of your business. There is no long-term benefit on making a sale based upon a USP you then ignore in all your transactions with the new client, you will very soon have a dissatisfied client.

Make sure all of your staff know your USP and how it affects all transactions with outside parties. Ensure all your staff know their job is to make good on the promise that is contained within your USP.

All staff should be extraordinarily courteous, empathetic, genuinely informative, sincere, and most important of all, they should offer supreme service. This should apply in dealing with anyone who comes into contact with your business, not just customers.

Every time something goes wrong your company has a chance to impress. Most customers accept that problems happen from time to time, but they want to feel sure that all problems will be dealt with cleanly and efficiently.

If someone calls to complain about a product or service it's vital that your company deals with the complaint in a courteous, efficient manner. Once the problem has been dealt with, always call the customer to ensure that everything is settled to THEIR satisfaction.

IDEA 59
BACK-END PRODUCTS.

If you do not have an effective back-end product, do yourself a favour and get one as soon as possible. In fact get your staff together today and start brainstorming some ideas.

Back-end products are essential to increasing both the average order value and the average order frequency. Back-end products are simply further products or services that can be sold to customers once they have made their first purchase.

Back-end products can either take the form of a wider product range or more expensive products in the same range, e.g. a de luxe and super de luxe model.

In order to provide maximum value to customers it is necessary to have a number of products that can be sold. Obtaining new customers is the expensive part of the whole process. Once you have a new customer on board it is essential to sell them further products.

With a good successful back-end product you can afford to lose money in acquiring new customers if you have to. Your back-end products cover the cost of acquiring new customers. If you can afford to lose money on the front-end how much easier will it be to acquire an increasing number of new customers?

Please remember that you must only ever sell and promote back-end products and services that are at least as good as your primary products and services in terms of value and quality.

IDEA 60
JOINT VENTURES.

Joint ventures are a method of obtaining back-end products or services to sell without the need to develop and manage the delivery of those services yourself. Consider the following example:

How many conservatory and window companies contact their customer once the job has been done? If my experience is anything to go by the answer is none. However, a client who has just had a new conservatory may well be in the market for other services such as a landscape gardener, decorator or someone selling indoor plants.

The conservatory company could simply agree a joint venture with companies supplying these services and then take a cut for the introduction. Most conservatory companies probably think they sell conservatories.

Your joint venture partners get incremental revenue they never would have had before, and the reputation they never would have had before. They can tap into your multi-million pound investment and goodwill to sell their product. This can be very powerful for all concerned.

IDEA 61
CLIENTS ARE EASY TO LOSE.

What are you doing to ensure that you do not lose any clients? Almost a ridiculous notion isn't it? We all know that every business will lose clients during the year. Part of the job of the sales force is to get out there and replace the clients that we know will be lost and then find a few more in order to grow the business.

Let me say up front that I agree. Any business is likely to suffer the loss of a few customers. Some will move away, go out of business or no longer require the products or services that you are selling. But what are you doing to ensure that you do not lose any other clients?

How much better off would you be if you continued to gain new clients at your current rate while you stopped losing clients unnecessarily?

I realise that I seem to be picking on mortgage providers but they do seem to be such a good source of what not to do at the present time.

Recently the fixed period on my house mortgage came to an end and hence it was time to look around. The interesting thing is that my existing lender (who will remain nameless) was willing to offer a new customer a better deal than they were willing to offer me. They forced me to go somewhere else by not offering me the best deal they had available.

There must be less administration costs in keeping an existing customer and they know I pay each and every month like a good little soldier, so why drive me away?

Are you doing something similar in your business? When was the last time that you offered your long-standing clients a special deal that was not open to new clients as a way of saying 'thank you' for doing business with you?

When you have lost a client do you routinely call and find out why they have left? These may be some of the most painful conversations you can have in your business but they may also be the most valuable. If you receive an honest answer from a dissatisfied client I suggest you send them a gift to say 'thanks' because they have just done you a great favour.

Finding out why clients leave will provide you with insights into the changes you need to make in order to improve your business. Improving your business will mean that you lose fewer clients in the future and it also becomes easier to attract new clients, all of which means that you will be wealthier in the future than you are today.

Begin today.

IDEA 62
QUALITY OF SERVICE.

I recently had an experience that brought home to me just how important it is to constantly review the quality of your service and to put yourself in the position of your customer.

My wife and I attended a dinner-dance. This was a regular event we attended each year to support our daughter. The venue had changed from previous years and will have to go un-named. Although the evening was very enjoyable with good company, the venue and food was probably the worst I have ever experienced.

The room was very cold, which did not please the ladies who were in evening dresses. The food was bland, overcooked and cold. In fact it must rank as one of the worst meals that has ever been put before me. I probably cooked better food when I first went to university and had to learn to cook.

The service was slow because there were not enough staff. My daughter has a part-time job as a waitress in a local hotel and thought that if the service was as poor in the hotel everyone would be sacked.

Once the speeches began some large fans started in the kitchen and it was difficult to hear the speakers. The staff claimed to be unable to turn the fans off.

How this organisation ever obtains repeat business is beyond my ability to understand. They now have another hundred very unhappy ex-customers. You can be sure that no one will recommend the establishment to friends and family.

It is clear that the management never consider their service from the point of view of the customer. They never experience the service they are providing. It may be possible they believe the service is a good one, but if that is the case they have very serious problems in all aspects of their lives.

Most businessmen rarely take the time to consider the quality of their product from the point of view of the clients. If they did put themselves in the position of their clients they would probably make changes.

When was the last time you considered the quality of your product from the point of view of your customer? I hope that you called the office last week in order to experience the service. I sincerely hope that you enjoyed the experience if you did make the call.

Why not persuade a friend to make a purchase from your company and report back on the experience? Then have that same friend make a complaint and see how they are treated. It is all too easy to become wrapped up in the day-to-day business and not consider the really important question of the service that you are providing to your customers.

How would you feel if you had to deal with your company?

IDEA 63
WHAT ARE YOU PROMOTING?

Without promotion, something terrible happens - NOTHING!

P.T. Barnum (1810-1891)
Entrepreneur

We are going to give a little thought to a few considerations concerning advertising. As a society we seem to have become conditioned by the idea that we must advertise even if it is only in Yellow Pages. Many small businesses spend a large proportion of their marketing spend on advertising.

Now here is the first idea for you: If your advertising is not working then stop doing it.

I know this sounds obvious but many people carry on advertising because they feel that they should. They have little real idea of how effective the advertising is but everyone else advertises so that must be the way to get business. There is another small problem: how do you know if the advertising is working?

This brings us to the next point: Measure all of your advertising.

If you do not measure the results you achieve from your advertising you will never know if it is effective or not. Even an advert in Yellow Pages is expensive if it never produces any leads that turn into clients. The results of all advertising should be measured so that the advertising can be tested and adjusted as necessary.

The final point to consider today is: Only use Direct Response advertising

There are two types of advertising - Direct Response and Brand Awareness Building.

You need to understand the difference. Brand awareness advertising is used by large companies such as Asda and washing powder manufactures. The idea is to increase awareness of a brand. Brand awareness advertising is expensive, uncertain and largely un-measurable.

The purpose of Direct Response advertising is, not unsurprisingly, to create a response. The type of response may vary depending upon your business but the major benefit of this type of advertising is that it is quickly measurable and hence can be easily tested and changed as necessarily.

So if you are spending money on advertising do yourself a favour and stop all Brand Building advertising and switch to Direct Response advertising.

IDEA 64
MARKETING NEVER WORKS.

"Unhappiness is not knowing what we want and killing ourselves to get it."

Don Herold

I was speaking to a business owner a few days ago who was having difficulty growing his business. Turnover had been static for a few years while costs had been creeping up as they do. Interestingly he claimed to have tried every marketing idea going and none of them had worked. He seemed to have arrived at the idea marketing was a waste of time because nothing worked, nothing allowed him to increase his turnover to the next level.

In one sense I sympathised with him because we have all been in a similar position, with some marketing ideas if not all marketing. How many people have tried direct mail? They spend large amounts of money preparing a letter, buying a mailing list, sending out the letters only to receive zero response. This is a painful experience. Being disheartened they conclude that direct mail does not work.

Point out to them that direct mail works for other businesses and they will inform you that it does not work in their industry. They know because they have tried it.

Then they try advertising. They hire a firm to create some expensive advertising which costs large amounts of money. The advertising is run in various media and they receive no enquiries. Once again they conclude that advertising does not work. Of course if you point out to them that advertising seems to work for other companies they will assure you that advertising does not work in their industry. They know because they have tried it.

Of course other companies are growing. Your turnover may be static or only increasing slowly, but other companies have turnover growing at 10%, 20% or even faster, so various marketing ideas must be working for them. If you have tried a number of marketing ideas and they did not work it is time to give up the idea that these ideas do not work in your industry. If you have tried everything and nothing works the more likely explanation is that your execution is faulty.

If you want to grow your business and none of the things you have tried have worked, or you wish to grow faster but do not know how then seek outside help. Ask yourself a simple question, "What is more important to me – being able to say I have tried everything and nothing works in my industry, or having a growing business?"

IDEA 65
A LESSON IN PERFUME

Yesterday I purchased some perfume for my wife's birthday. I do not make a habit of buying perfume but some things just have to be done. I tell you this not to demonstrate what a good and caring husband I am but because the whole experience provided a wonderful marketing lesson. Although I cannot help feeling that perfume is expensive for what you get this particular purchase would have been cheap at twice the price.

So what made the transaction worthwhile (apart from the pleasure my wife will gain from the perfume, of course)? Stay with me and find out.

1. The transaction started with a smiling, friendly sales assistant who made me feel safe and welcome; necessary because not many men really want to buy perfume. Do you make your customers feel welcome – at every contact- or do they struggle to get any attention?

2. She then asked the age of the person I was buying for and declared that I needed a sophisticated perfume and she had some she would recommend I choose from. How wonderful is this? In about 20 seconds she establishes what I want so she is not just selling any old perfume she is selling the solution to my problem. She has established some expertise because she knows the solution to my problem and I do not need to worry. She has flattered me in a subtle way because I must be a sophisticated person to be married to a woman who wears sophisticated perfume. She may show exactly the same perfumes to a man less than half

half my age who is buying for his girlfriend but that is not the point. How do you establish your expertise for your business?

3. She then produces two different perfumes for me to choose from. Why only two? Well there is no point in confusing me, is there? If I do not like either of the two she simply takes out another. In fact because she is the expert and is showing me perfume for a sophisticated person most men will just choose between the two. Do you throw the kitchen sink at your clients or just the products that will solve their problem?

4. Once I had chosen a perfume we moved onto the size of bottle. Three different sizes came out. Offer people two choices and most will take the cheaper option. Add a third more expensive choice and a large number of people will upgrade to the middle option because they do not wish to look cheap. This tactic increases the average transaction value. How can you use it in your business?

5. Next came the up-sell. Would I like to buy some body lotion? Having no idea what body lotion is I was foolish enough to express an interest. The interesting thing here is that she only took out one bottle size of body lotion while she undoubtedly had a range of sizes. Why only one size? Well the up-sell is geared to the original product. If a customer purchases the cheapest perfume bottle they are not going to purchase the most expensive body lotion. If someone has purchased the most expensive perfume they will probably purchase a more expensive bottle of body lotion. Why confuse the customer with too much choice? At least I had the sense to call a halt when she tried to sell me aftershave.

6. Next she offered to gift wrap the perfume for me. They are providing a small, but unexpected free bonus that is of negligible cost but has a real value to the customer. How are you going to use this idea in your business to improve the experience of purchasing from you?

7. When I collected the now gift-wrapped present the sales assistant included two free samples of aftershave. Again the cost is small but some customers will try the product and come back for more or perhaps the wife or girlfriend will like the product and come back for more. Are you able to include a free sample in each sale your company makes?

8. Finally the sales assistant was using a system and was either very well trained or good at her job, I suspect both. What marketing systems do you have in place and how much time do you spend training your staff?

It was worth making the purchase just to see a smoothly running system at work. The perfume was a nice bonus for my wife.

IDEA 66
PREPARE TO SELL.

If you are going to sell your business in a few years time would you like to double the amount you are going to receive at the time of sale?

"Not possible!" you might say.

Well, I am here to tell you it is possible.

Some of you will say, "Yes, BUT I cannot work any harder so I will not have time to double the value of the business".

Well, you can double the value of the business while doing less work.

The question you have to answer for yourself is: Am I prepared to give up my current way of managing the business in order to create something of greater value while giving myself more time and freedom?

If the answer is 'yes' then read on; if the answer is 'no' you probably have something very pressing to do with your time.

Now consider some of the fundamentals that will help you to increase the value of your business while having a better life for yourself. You can of course ignore these fundamentals if you wish, but doing so will cost you money. Are these ideas new and revolutionary? Of course not, because fundamentals are, well, fundamental. These ideas would have served your father just as well as they will help you and your children.

I would like to be able to say these ideas are all my own but that is not true, I just spend an unusual amount of time and money on my own education and hence I learn a few things along the way. The ideas have come from different places but the words are my own.

Important Fundamentals:

1. Make yourself redundant.
2. Ensure you have a quality product.
3. Marketing is the driver for all successful businesses.
4. Implement a simple marketing system and sales can increase exponentially.
5. All successful businesses make their real profits in the back-end.
6. To be successful over the long term you must adjust to the changing demands of the market.

All very simple isn't it? No rocket science here, but then I am not a rocket scientist. Although I have no proof I suspect that not five out of a hundred small businesses follow these principles. Even a large number of people who already know these things and could have written the above list do not actually use these ideas in their business.

IDEA 67
DOUBLE IN VALUE.

Would you like to double the value of your business over the next few years? Not possible? You may be right and then again you may be wrong. I am not talking about doubling your turnover in the next few years although that may be possible. Many companies will double turnover and hopefully profits over the next few years.

I am talking about doubling the value of your business, the amount you could sell it for. If you own your own business the amount it is worth is more important than just the size of your turnover or your profits.

Would you like to double the value of your business while working fewer hours and feeling less stress? Yes it is possible. In fact your long hours may be one of the things that is stopping you doubling the value of your business.

There are two ways to increase the value of an owner-managed business.

You can increase turnover and profits so that the business is larger and hence more valuable. Of course this requires that you double turnover and profits which you may feel is just not possible. No doubt you can see yourself increasing your business by 50% over the next three years but not 100%

You can also put systems in place so that the business will run without you. Work to make yourself redundant. I recently read some research carried out by a group of accountants that said a prospective company purchaser will pay up to 32.4% more for a company with good systems that does not require the day-to-day involvement of the owner. The figure is a bit precise (that is accountants for you!) but the principle is sound.

Just imagine, you put systems in place so that you do not have to work such long hours and you become wealthier at the same time.

Now imagine your business only increases in value by 50% because we work together to make you redundant and at the same time we only grow your business by 35%. I think we can manage that, don't you? Well, your business will double in value.

Can you put that extra money to good use when you finally come to sell?

Don't worry about having to give up work. Making yourself redundant just means you are not involved in all the daily nitty-gritty and can stand back from your business. You will be able to spend more time on strategic matters. You may even find you enjoy work again and recapture the excitement you felt when you first set up the business.

IDEA 68
CONTACT YOUR CLIENTS TODAY.

Simply put: how often do you contact your clients? No, I do not mean send them an invoice or make a sales call. How often do you contact them just to say hello, let them know you are thinking about them, provide some information that may be of use to them or just offer a discount on something for no other reason than because they are a customer?

There is a saying that, "people like to do business with people they know, like and trust." If you never keep in touch your customers will soon forget you.

Contact your customers at least once a month in order to remind them of your existence. They will not remember you just because they buy from you.

Ask a business owner why they lose customers and most will say because of price. Interestingly enough they usually arrive at this conclusion without ever going to the trouble of asking the customers they have lost.

Research shows that taken as a whole only 9% of customers are lost because of price issues. A further 14% are lost because the product or service does not meet requirements and a whopping 68% are lost because of a little thing called perceived indifference. In other words your customers leave because they do not think you care about them.

Like most businesses you have spent large amounts of money to gain your customers. Why allow them to leave simply because you do not stay in contact on a regular basis?

Who would you prefer to deal with – someone you feel you know or someone who just turns up wanting something from you?

IDEA 69
PRICE IS NOT VALUE.

When was the last time you stopped to consider the 'price' and the 'value' of the products you sell in your business? Not recently I suspect. Much marketing today confuses these two words.

A lot of advertising these days, especially for information products, talks about a product having a 'value of £27' (the amount is not important for this example), especially when it is being given away as a bonus.

If an information product only has a value of £27 why would I bother buying it? The time I would spend reading the product is worth more than the product itself. The people selling the product really mean it has a 'price' of £27. When someone purchases any product they believe the purchase will bring them more value than the amount they are required to pay. The value of a product also varies between people as well as with time and place

You may think I am splitting hairs but I am not. Whenever someone says your product is too expensive they really mean they are not convinced the 'value' exceeds the 'price' by a sufficient margin to make a purchase worthwhile.

Maybe the value does not exceed the price or perhaps your marketing message was not strong enough. Bear in mind that value is in the eye of the prospect.

The cost of this book you are reading is small, but the value to you could be huge if you just take one idea and apply it in your business. If your business is currently worth £1m and you double its value over the next couple of years as a result of the ideas gained from reading a few books then the value you have gained will be substantial.

The point is this: People will buy more of your product if they believe its value to them exceeds the price they must pay. The greater this differential the easier the sale will be.

Why not spend some time today brainstorming ways in which you can increase the value of your product substantially more than you increase the price? Consider creating two or three levels of product where value exceeds price by increasing amounts. You can then up-sell customers and prospects to the higher value product.

IDEA 70
KNOW YOUR CUSTOMER.

Yesterday I purchased a loaf of bread. You might be thinking this is hardly a momentous event worth writing about and certainly not worth your time reading but stay with me a little longer because the transaction had something to teach us all.

I have been shopping at a small bakery near where I live for about two years now. During that time the same few staff have been serving and I generally purchase the same thing, a loaf of granary bread that I ask to be sliced.

Why should yesterday's transaction be so interesting? Well it is interesting because I suddenly realised it was the same as every other transaction I have undertaken in that shop.

The staff know who I am and yet they always ask me what I want and always ask if I want it sliced. There is no apparent recognition of the fact that I have been making the same purchase at least once per week for the last two years. There has never been any attempt to sell me anything over and above the loaf of bread.

Why does this matter? Because when people are recognised even in a small way they feel as if they belong and will be more loyal in their purchasing.

Does any of this matter to your business? I think so.

How do you make your regular customers feel wanted? Do your staff know their names or anything about them? Do you recognise their contribution to your business in any way? We all wish to feel significant in some way, even a small way. How do you let your best customers know they are significant to your business?

If you have customers who make the same purchase each week or month why not put them on a contract at an improved price and then simply deliver the same order they would usually make? Give them the facility to change the order should they need to. When a competitor calls, your customer is likely to simply say they are on a contract for those products and you have safeguarded your position.

Recognise your customers in small ways and they are more likely to feel you care about them, buy more and stay longer.

IDEA 71
MAKE LIFE A LITTLE EASIER.

What are you doing to make it easier for your clients to purchase from you? It is all too easy to assume that our clients will continue to purchase from us. After all we supply a great product and they are bound to see that.

Why should they go anywhere else?

Consider your own situation: if someone came along and offered you a better price, what would you do?

If someone offered you a better product for the same price, what would you do?

If someone made your life easier, easier to purchase a product, easier to pay, easier to return if faulty, what would you do?

What little extra could you do to make life easier for your clients? One thing of which you can be certain is that there are a number of benefits that you could supply your clients that would have a high perceived value to them and a low cost to you. Start by asking your clients what they would like. If you do not ask you will never know. Then sit down with your staff and have a brain storming session to find things that you would like in relation to the goods or service that you provide.

No idea is too whacky. The ideas that seem impossible at first may be the best ideas to follow. If you can do the 'impossible' you will obtain a major marketing advantage over all of your competitors.

Make life easy for your all your clients' staff. The person who places the order is just as important as the person who takes delivery or the person who uses the product or the person who pays the cheque.

The more you help, the more you sell.

MAKE YOURSELF REDUNDANT

IDEA 72
FREE YOURSELF WITH DELEGATION.

For many people delegation is a simple matter of saying, "just do that" and expecting whatever 'that' is to get done. If you stop and give the matter a few moments thought you will realise you probably take this attitude quite a lot and it does not work.

If you doubt what I say, spend a few minutes thinking about how you deal with your children if you have any; if not, how do your friends deal with theirs. Simply telling children of any age what to do is not effective. If this approach does not work with your kids, why should it work with your staff?

One of the first skills all owner/managers should learn is how to delegate. Anyone who has started a business from scratch realises a time comes when they cannot do everything themselves. Every business that is growing reaches a size at which the owner cannot be everywhere and control everything and unfortunately the larger the business becomes the greater the problem gets.

If you own a business and you want it to grow then it is essential that you become selective over the things you do personally. You must delegate whether you want to or not.

For many people delegation is a simple choice between "you do it or I do it". Not surprisingly things are not quite that simple.

There are, in fact, seven levels of delegation you can choose from depending upon the task to be delegated, the experience of the person to whom you are delegating and the amount of your own time you wish to free up.

Be sure to choose the level of delegation most suitable at the time. Each succeeding level will require more trust on your part, leave you with less direct control and give you more time to do other things to develop your business

Level 1: "Just do exactly what I have told you to do". Not actually delegation at all.

Level 2: "Look into this and let me know the facts. I will decide what to do". Here you are asking for investigation and analysis. Little delegation as you are simply using your staff to gather information.

Level 3: "Investigate this and give me your recommendation along with the other alternatives and all the pros and cons. I will let you know if you can go ahead." You will check before anything is done. Can be used for training staff if you take the time to talk through their work and the reasons for your decision.

Level 4: "Take a look at this situation and let me know your decision. Wait for my go ahead before continuing". You are still retaining ultimate control although the other person is trusted to judge the various choices and make a good decision.

Level 5: "Decide and let me know your decision. Go ahead unless I say not to". This is the first level at which the other person is given some real trust and authority. This is also the first level at which you begin to save decent amounts of time.

Level 6: "Decide and take the necessary action but let me know what you did". The other person now has some real authority, you save even more time but still have the opportunity to correct a faulty decision without excessive delay.

Level 7 "Decide and take action. No need to tell me what you did". At this level the other person has maximum authority, maximum trust and you save maximum time.

It is time to give some thought to your relationship with your staff and which level of delegation you are using.

Try something different, train your staff, gain more control over your own time and start developing your business.

IDEA 73
WHY ARE YOU IN BUSINESS?

It is a sad fact but many people do not enjoy going to work. They live for the weekend when they are able to go out and 'enjoy' themselves. This often seems to me to be an unfortunate way to live your life. It is much better to enjoy your work and your weekend.

Although I do not enjoy everything I do in my business and, like most people, I have 'off' days I can genuinely say that I enjoy what I am doing.

I know a number of people will read this book and many will gain some benefit from it. Some people may even use this information to kick-start major changes within their business. I know I will never meet or speak to most of the people who read what I am now writing.

Of the many people I am able to touch with this work some will simply go away, others will become customers for the other products and services and a few will become consulting clients. I can make a small difference in the lives of many and perhaps a large difference in the lives of a few.

In case you run away with the idea that I am into peace, flower power and living the 'Good Life' (self sufficiency for those who are not in the UK or have never seen the programme of that name) I am not. I do intend to create and run a successful business and make money while I help other people.

I tell you this because you need to decide why you are in business. You might be in business to make a difference in people's lives, make large amounts of money and retire as early as possible or just live a better life.

Decide why you are in business and then create a business that brings you whatever it is you want. A business can probably be whatever you want it to be, with the proviso that you must make a profit at some point in time. The first step is to decide what you want it to be.

IDEA 74
WHAT IS YOUR BUSINESS?

The next time you meet some independent business owners at a networking event I guarantee that a question you'll be asked, and will ask repeatedly is: "What do you do?"

Now when you hear this question listen very carefully to the answer, including the answer you give yourself. The answer will always take a similar format. People always answer with something along the lines of: "I am in conservatories, kitchens, widgets or whatever the business is."

You might be wondering why this matters.

If you currently have a business that turns over £2,000,000 making conservatories and you wish to double the size of that business you need to stop thinking that you are in the conservatory business.

Your company is in the conservatory business.

Your business is managing and growing your company.

When you think of yourself as being in the conservatory business you almost automatically become heavily involved in the day-to-day activities of your business.

If you truly wish to grow your business you must step back from the day-to-day activities and put systems in place to make sure they happen without you. It was Michael Gerber who taught us that any business owner who must go into the office each day has a job, not a business. Not only that, you have the worst job in the company. You have large amounts of money tied up and you cannot walk away and get another job.

If you want your business to enhance your life rather than detract from it you must begin to build a business that will get along quite well without you. You must start to MAKE YOURSELF REDUNDANT. Create a business where you can work part-time, or full-time as you please. Start and make running your business your business.

Many years ago I remember talking to the finance director of a private company who told me that as far as the owner was concerned the year was over. The company had a December year-end and our conversation was taking place in March and yet the owner already considered the year to be over. Why did he do that?

This businessman had put people and systems in place so the business would run without him on a day-to-day basis. He was now spending most of his time thinking about what the business would be doing next year and the year after that. The nice thing about concerning yourself with what the business will be doing next year and the year after is that you can do a substantial amount of your work lying on a beach or sitting around a pool or on a golf course.

Would you prefer a business where you have to go into work tomorrow or one where you have the people and systems in place to run the business in your absence for a few weeks or months?

IDEA 75
FREE UP YOUR TIME.

If you wish to be free to develop your business it is essential that you have free time during the day. Most business owners are the first in, last out and spend every minute of the day busy, busy, busy.

Suggest to these owners steps they should take to grow their business and they complain they do not have the time. For most people this is true. Most business owners are involved in everything that is going on in the business. Few decisions are taken without their input, little can happen without their say so. No wonder they are reluctant to take a holiday, who knows what will happen while they are away?

Just in case you were wondering I know what it feels like because I have done exactly the same in the past. Trust me on this. If you are involved in all the detail of your business you need to stop. If it does not kill you it will stop you growing your business and having a better life.

Most business owners feel they should set an example by being the first in and the last out. After all if they do not how can they expect anyone else to. Unfortunately they have a lot of time that needs to be filled and most of them do so by becoming involved in the detail.

It is understandable that business owners become involved in all the minutiae because they started out dealing with everything and they are now unable to let go.

I have got some news for you that none of your staff will tell you. They would like you to take a week off and not phone the office. They would be pleased if you took time off to play golf, it would give them time to catch up with the work they are unable to get done while you are in the office.

When you are involved in all the detail you simply prevent the smooth flowing of the systems you ought to be setting up.

Here is an exercise to show the extent of your problem and provide the information you require to begin and deal with it.

For the next two weeks keep a timesheet. If you followed my earlier suggestion and kept a record of everything you do for a two week period you can now use that information for a further exercise. If you did not record your activities earlier then please do so over the next two weeks. Record everything you do in six-minute blocks. Everything you do from the time you arrive at work until the time you leave should be recorded. Don't say it is too difficult because if you were a solicitor that is precisely what you would be doing.

At the end of two weeks you are going to analyse your time – no surprises there but the way you are going to analyse it may be.

Start by drawing up a simple organisation chart. Not a chart of your organisation but a chart of a typical organisation. Every company will have a managing director who should be looking to the future of the business. There will then be three functional heads in:

- Production
- Finance/Admin

- Sales/Marketing

Under Sales/Marketing will be a sales manager and then salesmen. Under Finance/Admin will be a purchase ledger, sales ledger etc. I am sure you get the picture.

Now go through and analyse your two weeks. Put everything you have done in the last two weeks into one of the boxes you have created. You can now see how much time you have spent acting as salesman, sales manager and sales director. You will be able to identify how much time you have spent working at a low level on the shop floor and how little time you have spent doing the job of managing director.

Your next step is to start putting systems in place to ensure the low-level detail work you are currently doing is getting done without you and free up time to do the managing director's job.

Free up time and start to grow your business.

Idea 76
Put systems in place.

If you want your business to enhance your life rather than detract from it you must start by putting systems in place. I fully realise that many people start a business because they do not like the systems they are forced to follow when working for a large organisation.

I fully understand how you feel. Over the years I have introduced many systems and then felt myself frustrated by having to follow them. The fact is however that systems *will set you free* and *substantially increase* the value of your business.

Systems will reduce the need for you to be involved in the day-to-day running of your business. Systems will ensure that every time a customer contacts your business the experience they have is the same.

Providing people with an identical experience each time they contact your business will keep them coming back – as long as the experience is a good one of course. Most people like to feel comfortable; they like to know that the experience they are going to have will be familiar.

One of the things that has made McDonalds so successful is the fact that everyone knows what they are getting when they go to eat there. The food and the experience is the same regardless of the restaurant they eat in. The system is probably Ray Kroc's lasting contribution to the company.

Why do you go to the same hairdresser every time? Because it is familiar and you know what the experience will be like. You would be very unhappy if a different person cut your hair each time you went to a particular hairdresser.

You expect the same person to cut your hair, you expect to sit in the same chair and be offered a cup of coffee. You expect your hairdresser to know how you like your hair cut, you do not wish to explain yourself every time you go. Boring perhaps, but you know what to expect every time you go.

Create a good, consistent experience for everyone who comes into contact with your business and its value will increase.

When you come to sell your company I assume you would like to achieve the maximum price for it. If you are intimately involved in all aspects of the business it will be worth substantially less than if you can simply hand over the keys to the new owner and walk away.

A business that runs effectively, efficiently and continues to grow without the need for the owners to be involved on a daily basis will always be worth more than a business that requires large amounts of managerial input.

When you are starting to implement systems start at the bottom of your organisation chart and work your way up. Begin with any work you are currently doing that really belongs at a lower level in the organisation and create a system to ensure it is done without you having to do it. This will also free up your time and put you in a better position to implement more systems.

Try having your managers record their time for two weeks and then identify the work they do each week that should be carried out at a lower level then take steps to ensure it is.

Making your objective to take a month off while knowing that when you come back, the business will be waiting for you in good shape and probably making more profit than it was at the start of your holiday.

IDEA 77
CREATE A PLAN.

Decide what you wish to do and how big you want your business to be and start moving towards it.

Once you have developed your plan stick to it. This does not mean you will not change your plan from time to time, of course you will. As your business grows and you grow with it you will learn more and realise your plan has to change, but develop a plan and start moving and stick to it.

I challenge you to decide where you want to go with your business, create a plan and stick to it.

You can thank me later.

Here are a few elements you need to consider for your plan:

1. What activities are you going to create systems for?
2. How are you going to involve your staff?
3. What marketing systems are you going to create?
4. What do you need to know?

You might be wondering why I have slipped the last item onto the list. The simple answer is that your business will only be a big as you are. It does not matter how much your turnover is at the present time, if you wish to double the turnover you must do something differently.

As a business moves from £1m to £2m or from £3m to £6m turnover it faces different challenges and problems and has to be managed differently. If you are only really capable of managing a business with a £1m turnover you are going to find it very difficult to create a business with a £6m turnover.

The first thing that has to change on the journey is you. You set the tone for your business, you decide where it is going, you set the tone for the way in which staff treat each other and the way staff treat customers. Your own ongoing education and learning is a key part of moving your business forward.

Growing your business is a journey to be enjoyed.

IDEA 78
DECISIONS ARE PUSHED DOWN THE HIERARCHY AS FAR AS POSSIBLE.

If you are serious about growing your business then you must start by freeing up some of your own time to do the things that will take you forward. Most managers spend large amounts of time engaged in activities that should be delegated. Why is this? I suspect because we all have times when we need to feel able to do the things we are doing.

Unfortunately this way of working is bad for the organisation and bad for you. Decisions and activities should take place at the lowest possible level within the organisation. At this level the activities will probably be carried out most effectively and the organisation will run most efficiently.

When a decision that should be taken at a low level is taken at a high level a number of people become involved. The person who should take the decision or carry out the action is involved, their boss is involved and possibly their boss's boss is involved. In this situation large amounts of time is wasted, staff become frustrated and the service that is provided to customers suffers.

An efficient and effective organisation is one in which decisions and actions take place at the lowest possible level. A further major benefit you will receive is the freedom to concentrate more time and energy on developing the business.

In order to free up your own time try the following exercise

If you kept the time sheet mentioned previously you can also use the information to decide the activities you are going to delegate in order to free up time to develop your business. If there are some activities that could be delegated but you are reluctant to do so because you need to be sure they are carried out correctly consider the following:

- Do you want a particular result or do you want things done the way you do them?

- Someone else may see a better way of achieving the same result if you give them the opportunity.

- Put a system in place to keep you informed without you being actively involved.

- Free up some time and grow your business.

IDEA 79
ASK YOUR STAFF.

If you wish to create a business that will run quite happily without you, there are going to have to be a number of changes and improvements.

You may be a superb business person but it is highly unlikely you are able to think of all the improvements that could be made to your business.

Some of the best ideas for improving your business will come from your staff. You simply have to ask them. You must first create an atmosphere in which your staff feel able to offer up suggestions without them being taken as criticism.

Your staff also need to feel that any suggestions they make will be taken seriously and acted upon where appropriate.

Any member of your staff is capable of making suggestions to improve your business, but they will only do so if they feel comfortable doing so.

You may find that a few good brainstorming sessions will provide enough good ideas for improving your business to keep you busy for the next six months.

IDEA 80
THE DAFFODIL PRINCIPLE
By Jaroldeen Asplund Edwards

Several times my daughter had telephoned. "Mother, you must come and see the daffodils before they are over." Finally, I promised, reluctantly. I'd driven only a few miles when the road was covered with wet, grey fog. As I slowly executed the hazardous mountain turns, I was praying to reach the turning. When I finally walked into Carolyn's house, I said, "Forget the daffodils, Carolyn! There is nothing that I want to see badly enough to drive another inch in this weather!"

"I'll drive," Carolyn offered. In a few minutes, we were back on the rim-of- the-world road heading over the top of the mountain.

We parked in a small parking lot adjoining a little stone church. I saw a pine needle-covered path, and an inconspicuous, hand-lettered sign saying "Daffodil Garden". I followed Carolyn down the path. Then we turned a corner. It looked as though someone had taken a great vat of gold and poured it down every crevice and over every rise. Even in the mist, the mountainside was radiant, clothed in massive drifts and waterfalls of daffodils. A charming path wound through the garden with several resting stations, with Victorian wooden benches and great tubs of tulips. It didn't matter that the sun wasn't shining. Five acres of flowers!

"But who...?" I asked Carolyn.

"Just one woman," Carolyn answered. "That's her home."

On the patio we saw a poster. "Answers to the Questions I Know You Are Asking" was the headline. The first answer was simple. "50,000 bulbs." The second was, "One at a time, by one woman, two hands, two feet, and very little brain." The third was, "Began in 1958."

There it was. The Daffodil Principle. For me it was a life-changing experience. I thought of this woman, who, more than thirty five years before, had begun one bulb at a time to bring beauty and joy to an obscure mountain top. No shortcuts, loving the slow process of planting. She had changed her world. Her daffodil garden taught me about learning to move toward our goals and desires one step at a time, learning to love the doing, learning to use the accumulation of time.

"It makes me sad in a way," I admitted. "What might I have accomplished if I had thought of a wonderful goal thirty-five years ago and worked away at it all those years. My wise daughter responded, "Start tomorrow."

IDEA 81
THE WORLD REWARDS
ACTION NOT THOUGHT.

Well actually I think the world rewards thought followed by action but either way action is necessary. The first thing you need to do is decide if you do wish to double the value of your business while having more free time. What would that be worth to you? What could you do with the extra time and money and are you willing to make a few changes to get it?

Consider the following idea and see if you are willing to adopt it: I am willing to do today what most others will not, so I can live a life tomorrow that most others cannot.

IDEA 82
HOW MUCH DO YOU
DO EACH DAY?

Let me ask you a question, "How much productive time do you spend working on your business?"

I recently read some information claiming that the Chief Executives of Fortune 500 companies spent 28 minutes per day on productive work. This set me thinking about my own business.

Work is productive when it will move your business forwards e.g. working on a marketing campaign, installing systems to ensure work is carried out without your involvement. Reading letters, making phone calls, most meetings are not productive. Reading this book is not productive. Your time would only become productive if you started to apply the idea it contains.

So, how much productive time do you spend in your business?

Try keeping a time sheet for the next two weeks and see how horrified you are.

What if you manage one productive hour each day, or five hours per week or 240 hour per year. You are trying to grow your business on 240 hours per year. You are never going to reach the point where all of your time is spent productively but what if you could arrange one extra hour per day? Do you think this would make a major difference to your life? You could make a substantial difference by doubling the amount of productive time you spend each day.

How do you increase your productive time?

Record everything you do over the next two weeks then stop doing the things that do not need to be done and start to delegate tasks that can be delegated. Free up your time and spend it productively on your own business.

IDEA 83
CREATE A REAL BUSINESS.

If you wish to create a "real" business where do you start? What is a "real" business?

A "real" business is a business that will continue to grow with or without you. You can walk away from a "real" business, take a month or three months off and know that when you return the business will be larger and more profitable than when you left.

If you cannot take a few months off from your business you do not own a business you own a job and you have the worst job in the company.

You have to be there every day (no sick days for you!), you have all the responsibility, most of your wealth is tied up in the business, you cannot go and look for another job tomorrow and you are dependent on the sale of the business to provide your pension.

You are the only person in your business who is locked in and cannot walk away. You are lonely because you are the owner. You are the only person who cannot spend time griping about the company, other staff and the boss.

The worst thing about most businesses is that the owner works for a complete lunatic. If you doubt that you work for a lunatic try writing a specification and advert for your job. How easy do you think it would be to find someone to apply?

All of this remains true if you are self-employed or have a hundred staff.

Now we have cleared that up it is time to ask yourself a question, "Do you wish to create a 'real' business, a business that brings you freedom and enhances your life or would you rather continue as you are?"

So what is the first thing you need to do?

Start by giving up on the idea that you should do, or know about, everything in your business, or even anything in your business. Understand that doing technical or co-ordinating work does not create a business it creates a job.

Begin by recording how you spend your time then analyse your time to see how much is spent on a job, either as a technician or a co-ordinator and how much you spend as a strategist developing a business.

A friend returned a phone call yesterday. He apologised for not calling earlier but "things had been hectic as usual" for the past few days. If your life is always hectic or you are wondering why you cannot grow your business the starting point is quite simply how you choose to spend your time.

Time is all you have got. The way you use your time and the activities you engage in will determine if you create a "real" business and how large it will become.

Creating a real business is about developing systems and being involved in specific projects designed to move your business forward. You will not be able to do this while you are spending nearly all of your time on technical or co-ordinating roles.

The secret to building a company is not in doing your own work but in creating a system to ensure it gets done.

IDEA 84
WHAT IS YOUR LIMITING FACTOR?

I am sure you have all heard of the concept of limiting factors. In relation to your business this simply means "what is stopping you achieving the objectives you have set for yourself or your business?"

I feel sure you can think of a long list, or maybe in your case it is a very short list. Are you short of finance, just cannot seem to be able to hire good people, cannot find clients, cannot keep clients?

Of course we all know there will be as many reasons than there are people reading this and if the number of readers doubled then the number of reasons would more than double.

Everyone who owns or manage a business is beset by a myriad of problems and difficulties.

But what if I were to tell you there is only one limiting factor within your business would you believe me? Would you even want to believe me? When I tell you what that limiting factor is will you stop reading and unsubscribe? Well I am going to have to take that risk.

The one limiting factor within your business is YOU. That's right. You are the reason your business has grown to the size it is and you are the reason it is not growing as fast as you might like.

Research carried out in 2002 concluded that two thirds of owner/managers of SMEs (small and medium sized enterprises) hoped to retire before they were 60.

- 82% of owners over 56 do not have a written plan to prepare their business for sale.
- Only 22% of owners claim they are very confident they will be in a comfortable financial position by the time they retire.

These owners really have no one to blame but themselves. If they do nothing then nothing will happen.

The only thing that will enable your business to move forward is if you move forward. In order to move forward you must learn new things and apply them in your business.

What books are you reading? Where else are you going to get new ideas except from reading and talking to people?

What, no time to read books and try new ideas?

Well here is the first idea for you. Make time. Start and create a business that gives you the time to look for new ideas.

It's what you don't know that you don't know, that makes all the difference.

In the last three months has your business made any serious progress towards your goals? You do have a goal don't you?

In most SME failures, a key reason is the owners not recognising weaknesses and not seeking help to deal with them.

You are the limiting factor within your business. When you grow your business can grow. What are you reading and who are you speaking to?

What should you do now?

Whatever you do, make certain you do something. There are a number of ideas contained within this book that you can apply to your business today. Take one idea and implement it today. Once you are obtaining value from that idea choose another and implement that one also.

Your business has within it potential which is just sitting, waiting for you to do something. Start today.

Just as importantly take time to step back from your business and consider where you are now and where you would like to be in five years time. Once you know where you wish to go, start taking a few steps in that direction.

Whatever you choose to do I wish you every success.

Stuart Lockley